ENDORSEMENTS

"In the midst of bullets flying and paralyzing fear gripping her soul, Jessika Tate heard the Lord say, "Jessika, if you can't trust me in moments like this, then I can't trust you in places like this."

These are sobering words for a missionary called to the dark places of the earth. In this wonderful story, *Trials to Triumph*, Jessika Tate discovers that the measure of impact on the world around her will be equal to the absolute trust in God that flows from within her. New assignments will always require new levels of trust. She discovered this reality the hard way, as bold faith stands on the shoulders of quiet trust.

Trials to Triumph is a transparent story of courage and a near fatal collapse, followed by the wonderful healing grace of a perfect Father. This story will encourage, challenge and inspire the reader to greater faith and trust to fulfill our God-given assignment in this world."

—BILL JOHNSON
BETHEL CHURCH, REDDING, CA
AUTHOR OF *THE WAY OF LIFE* AND *RAISING GIANT-KILLERS*

"I have the privilege of week after week hearing amazing stories of people's lives being changed by the goodness of God. Jessika has been a part of our family here at Bethel, and her story and testimony are one of the most exceptional ones we've seen.

Trials to Triumph is a game-changer as it unravels any perception that God isn't good and it releases hope into impossible situations that only God can heal and restore. Her story is one that will not only bring joy to you but more importantly, reveals the goodness of God more then we thought."

—ERIC JOHNSON
BETHEL CHURCH, REDDING, CA

"As a minister for over four decades, I am always on the lookout for emerging leaders who could be the forerunners of the next wave of revival. Jessika Tate is one of these leaders. In her new book, Trials to Triumph, Jessika speaks with unusual maturity and wisdom about the trauma she experienced as a missionary in war torn countries.

She also declares with amazing clarity, how the power of God touched her life to remove the trauma and restore her life and ministry to a greater level than before. This book will grab you and shock you, but it will also speak to the areas of trauma, pain, and disappointment in your life and guide you to an interaction with the Holy Spirit that will give you beauty for ashes, the oil of joy for mourning and the garment of praise for the spirit of heaviness. This book is a must-read!"

—DR. MICHAEL BRODEUR
AUTHOR, SPEAKER AND CATALYTIC CONSULTANT.
PASTORSCOACH.COM

"Trials to triumph is not only a book, but it's a journey. A journey through seasons, a journey from hardship into victory. Many will say they follow Christ, but would they follow Him into a war zone? Jess is a woman who has both followed and surrendered her life, and is living in that glorious experience. That's what I believe this book will be for you: a glorious experience. One of faith, surrender and victory."

—JENNY KUTZ
LOVE TO THE NATIONS

"Jessika has given us tools of overcoming through deeply painful experiences and setbacks in her own life and how God reached out and miraculously touched her and began to heal the broken pieces of her life.

Jessika is candidly honest and weaves in biblical understanding with wisdom and wit to open up our hearts to God's relentless love that redefines what success looks like when we look like a failure, or worse yet—a nothing.

She holds out her hand offering us a way out of the effects of pain by embracing our struggle to know Him in the midst of what doesn't make sense. He is good—no matter what. End of story. How we process this is the essence of this book.

Her surrender to God is so fresh and real as she says, "It's not my job to fix the mess; it's my responsibility to yield to the One who is really good at fixing things."

Whatever you do, buy this book and devour all of the incredible nuggets that will help you on the journey of trusting God when you feel like giving up and to prepare you for the many ups and downs in life. It's full of humor, honesty, and thought-provoking discovery. It's a keeper."

—THERESA DEDMON
BETHEL PASTOR
BETHEL CREATIVE ARTS DIRECTOR
AUTHOR OF BORN TO CREATE

"It has been a blessing to know and do life with Jessika the last few years. We've watched her truly seek God's way in handling challenging situations, but what has been even more beautiful is watching her go after God's heart for social justice. Our prayer is that as you read this book you will not only be encouraged, but will be challenged to dream bigger with God and feel His heart for the broken and the needy."

—WILL AND MUSY HART
IRIS MINISTRIES

"Jessika is a woman yielded to God. Not for a gospel of pleasure but to truly die to her will in order for her to live the life of Christ in her. She gladly counted the cost and went into the worn, torn nation of DR-Congo where in her obedience to Jesus to GO, she suffered the trauma of the call. Full of pain and believing she was a failure, she hit rock bottom and had to leave Congo to get help. She wrongly believed that returning to the US would fix her problem, but the anxiety and pain increased. In her desperation, Jesus took her to a place of vulnerability and trust in Him where she was willing to embrace the journey of healing and restoration and restore lost hope.

In *Trials to Triumph*, Jess challenges us in our own journey of trust in Jesus and His power to heal, save, and deliver. She embraced the cup of suffering part of the gospel message so rarely talked about or shared in the Body of Christ in our western paradigm, but so needed. Jesus said, "In this world you will have trouble, but take heart, I have overcome the world." She gives hope to many who are also suffering with PTSD and other negative conditions, giving them hope for their own freedom and to become the wounded healers that restore the body of Christ to health."

SENIOR LEADER, CATCH THE FIRE RALEIGH-DURHAM
PRESIDENT OF *CATCH THE FIRE*

"I was present the day God healed Jessika. During worship that morning, one of our team came over to me and asked if she could bring Jessika into the middle of the room and dance around her. She had never danced around anyone before this and had only recently stepped out to dance for the first time maybe a month before. I told her that if she got permission from Jessika first, then she could go for it! After she had danced around her, myself and a few others gathered around Jessika to pray for her as her tears fell rapidly to the floor.

When I had first met Jessika, she was nothing at all like her profile picture on social media portrayed her to be as a preacher woman. The Jessika I first met was dead inside. After she was healed that day and God continued to bring her back to life, I realized what a powerful miracle God had done. She was a completely different person than the Jessika I had originally met. As God's love continued to restore her soul, I saw more of the significant call of God on her life that the enemy was afraid of.

After witnessing God's healing power bring Jessika back to life, I invited her to share her story in several meetings. Every time her testimony is released, I see God heal broken minds and hearts, restore hope, inspire courage, and unlock people's destinies in a powerful way. I pray God does the same in your life as you receive this gift from her heart wrapped up in this book.

Jessika is one of the most humble, passionate, and unoffendable people I know. She has given her yes to Jesus no matter what the cost. Her life and her story are inspiring and convicting. As you read Jessika's vulnerable account of how Jesus led her through the storms of life and held her hand all the way through, I pray that you experience the healing power of the Holy Spirit and are filled with great hope and courage as you keep your eyes on Jesus and step into all that He has for you."

—JENNIFER A. MISKOV, PH.D.
FOUNDING DIRECTOR OF DESTINY HOUSE,
WRITING IN THE GLORY, AND SCHOOL OF REVIVAL

Working to heal from trauma is full of hardship and learning how to overcome or cope with it is a process. Jessika Tate shares her raw experience struggling with PTSD and how God healed her mentally, physically, and emotionally. The symptoms she describes gives readers an idea of what living in the midst of PTSD is like for an individual, especially on the mission field. PTSD effects millions of adults each year and the impact goes beyond the individual experiencing these symptoms. Tate writes about her struggles with loved ones, friendships, and others during this difficult season of life that still impacts her today. Coping with PTSD takes courage and an army of people battling the storms with an individual, whether through prayer, being physically present, and/or emotionally supportive, is how God designed community to look like.

This is a book about struggle, hope, and God's victory. It will help people know they are not alone and encourage others to keep fighting the good fight. It is a reminder that there is nothing too big for God and He is always present in the midst of our trials and triumphs. No trauma can overpower God's purpose for His people and Jessika's story is a living example of just that.

—MACY WALTZ, PHD, LPC

Jessika Tate is dear to my heart. As part of our *Agape Freedom Fighters* ministry team we look forward to spending time with her and hearing of her latest adventures with Jesus. She is unstoppable. When I look at Jessika I see the light of Christ shining on a hill to illuminate an entire generation with the love, truth and tools of Jesus to bring them into their destiny.

Her latest release, *Trials to Triumph* is the story of our God of miracles overtaking her own life of trauma and bringing her into His marvelous healing light where not a shred of darkness remains. Jessika's ability to connect to her readers emotionally and spiritually is renown and in every chapter you will find nuggets of wisdom and practical applications to overcome every obstacle in your own life. I pray that as you read *Trials to Triumph*, you too will encounter the power of the Holy Spirit and experience true transformation in Christ just as Jessika did.

—REVEREND JOANNE MOODY,
AGAPE FREEDOM FIGHTERS

TRIALS TO TRIUMPH

TRIALS TO TRIUMPH

THE HEART OF GOD IN YOUR MOST PAINFUL MOMENTS

JESSIKA TATE

DEDICATION

I dedicate this book to my nephew Alister and all of my spiritual sons and daughters both now and in the future.

May every scar from battles won and lost represent ones you won't have to fight. I pray that you learn from the successes and failures of those who have gone before you so that you will press even further into all that He has dreamed for you.

CONTENTS

Acknowledgments   xvii

1. Where it Begins   1
2. Season of Bliss   7
3. Gunshots Rang Out   11
4. Tribulations Come   17
5. The Forgotten Ranch   23
6. The Gift of Pain   27
7. Church Masks   33
8. Made for Community   43
9. Will You Leave, Too?   51
10. Time to Move   61
11. Not What I Hoped For   67
12. Dance Over Me   71
13. God's Presence or Promise?   75
14. God on Trial   79
15. Divine Set-Ups   87
16. Make the Enemy Pay   91
17. Time to Let Go   99
18. Redefining Success   103
     Epilogue   107

About the Author   111

ACKNOWLEDGMENTS

Katharina Welt: Your yes saved my life. I don't know how you ever say thank you enough for something like that, but know your act of obedience will forever be etched in my history with God.

Kayce Strader: This book literally would not be a reality without your help. You have been a faithful friend for over a decade, a source of wisdom, encouragement, and all of the best things in a friend. So thankful for our girl "goat" tribe!

Maegan Rossow: You not only helped with the book, you helped me through the most difficult season of my life. You have never stopped believing in me since day one. No one person has called me higher, challenged me more, or shown me so much mercy and grace as you have. You embody love and have taught me what true friendship is.

My family: For never giving up on me even when you had a

million reasons to do so. Mom, Dad, Nic, Jake, Alister, you're my people forever.

Sarah W. Howe: You were a gift from the Lord that came at just the right moment. I could not ask for a better therapist or a better friend.

Jen Miskov: You convinced me this was a story that needed to be told and walked with me throughout the vulnerable journey. Thanks for believing in me and this book.

Jedida Gomes, Hailie Fields, Joy Murphy, Melissa Moss, Macy Waltz, thanks for being the early supporters.

My BSSM interns for 2019, Lucy, Sam, Kat: Thank you for believing in this project and not letting me throw it away no matter how many times I wanted to!

There are way too many pastors, leaders, and friends to mention from the Bethel environment that deserve to be mentioned for helping me through such a difficult season. You know who you are and I am forever grateful.

And finally to the random man who prophesied this book into existence: You gave me the courage I needed to finally put this story out there. I don't know your name, but you'll forever be part of this story.

1

WHERE IT BEGINS

"WELCOME, WE ARE GLAD YOU ARE HERE," THE MISSIONARY SAID when I got off the plane in Sudan. "Feel free to walk around on the base, but do *not*, do *not ever* go off the path when you're off base. It hasn't been swept for mines, and if you step on one, you will blow up. At night, you will probably have demonic encounters. There is a lot of spiritual activity in this region. If you cannot handle it yourself, you can come get me for help. Come, I'll show you where you can set up your tent."

This journey did not begin the day gunshots rang out. It did not begin the day the nightmares started, or even when the suicidal thoughts came. No, this journey began when Jesus interrupted my life at sixteen years old.

It may sound dramatic, but if I started with the war stories and did not explain how I got there, you might get the wrong idea about me. First, you would probably think I'm fearless. Trust me, I'm not. You would easily find this out if you ever saw me try to climb a ladder or hike anything larger than a hill. Inevitably, I would end up belly crawling to stay as close as possible to my friend named "gravity" and we would all put the fearless nonsense behind us. I don't really believe in fearless people. I do, however, believe in a love that supersedes fear. Second, without hearing some of my history with Him, you might not fully understand the weight of the pain or confusion of the trials that came into my life. Make no mistake about it, I was knocked to my knees and ready to quit, but let's just start from the beginning.

I did not want to become a "war zone" missionary. If you would have told me that I would be jumping around the globe into some of the most dangerous places of war, rape, and violence, I would have laughed in your face. Like so many of my friends in the work that I've done, I did not lay in bed as a child dreaming of nations. I mean, I was a Texan. Excuse me, I *am* a Texan. And Texans are mostly content to live forever in Texas. You only understand this fully if you're a Texan.

At 16 years old, I had gone out to a party and drank too much on a Friday night. As I was lying in my bed, my brother was taking care of my friend who was "under the weather" in the bathroom. (This is the point in the story my poor mother shakes her head and secretly wishes she could go back and spank 16-year-old me. I don't blame her. Shout out to all the parents out there that aren't giving up on their kids. Listen, He hears you. Do not give up. You never know when or how He'll sweep in.)

I don't remember much about the night up until this moment. I was lying there in my bed and I heard my name audibly: "Jessika." (Let me also assure you that God is not in the habit of speaking to me audibly, though I sure wouldn't mind if He did.) Not being used to God speaking to me, I assumed it was my brother in the other room and yelled back. He rushed into the room and told me that I needed to quiet down or I would get in trouble. A second time I heard my name, "Jessika," and a second time I yelled back at my brother. Same response. Finally a third time, I heard my name and this time I just had a simple thought: "What if this is God?"

That question is the moment my story really begins. This moment is forever captured in my history with Him. This is the moment that no trial, no turmoil, no lie, no man, no demon can ever take from me. He spoke to me and said, "Jessika, I set before you life and death, and I plead with you to choose life!"

I had an unshakeable realization in that moment that if I did not give God my life that instant, then I would be choosing death. It was either life with Him or death without Him. Since that day, I knew this wasn't something I could do half way. He was either deserving of every breath or none at all. His words demanded a response. It could not be half-hearted or nominal—it required my total devotion.

I gave my life to Jesus that day, and every single day since then has been marked by that moment, by that choice. There is not one area of my life that hasn't been touched and influenced by that decision. Within just a few days, I found myself constantly on my face weeping, praying, screaming out my commitment. Moments where I was so overwhelmed by who He was that all I could do was pray what I call "dangerous prayers." I used to call them stupid prayers. Truth be told, I still occasionally think of them that way. Mine sounded like this: "God, I'll go anywhere. I'll do anything for You; take me where no one else wants to go!" My only natural response to His ultimate sacrifice was the total sacrifice of my own life for Him. All for all. I meant what I prayed; I just didn't have one clue what it meant.

I began going to Africa while I was in college and quickly fell in love with every nation I went to. I felt like I was living the dream

I didn't know I should dream. It was truly better than I had imagined, until one day God asked me to do something absurd.

I had a map set out on my bed, just like my hero Corrie Ten Boom used to do, asking Him where we were going next. This time as I sat there praying, I heard in my spirit so clearly, "Sudan." When He first said it, I thought it was in South America (I was not so good with geography). I got a little excited about going to a new continent and I marched into my living room, giddy to tell my brother about my next adventure.

"I'm going to Sudan," I said. My brother looked up at me and flatly replied, "No, you are not." I thought that was an odd reaction, but I can be feisty and simply said, "YES, I AM. God just said so!" My brother pulled up an article to show me. He said, "Jessika, have you heard of Darfur?"

Of course, I'd heard of Darfur. It was all over the news. A horrible famine and genocide taking place along with protests all through the States petitioning for our government to get involved. I told him yes, I'd heard of Darfur, and then he dropped the bomb: "Jessika, Darfur is in Sudan."

It knocked the wind out of me. One moment, I was so excited to go to a new continent, and the next, I thought God was sending me to Sudan to die. I didn't even know that people went and did missions in places like that. No one in their right mind actually goes where the bullets are flying and machetes are hacking. Right?! I knew in Rwanda that the majority of pastors and ministries fled as soon as the genocide broke out. Supposedly, there were a few crazy, albeit brave, heroes who stuck around. I loved those stories, but I was no hero. I was not trying to get my name in one of the books for martyrs. I'd prefer to tell my grandchildren about the adventures I've lived, not have them reading about them in my journals after I died.

Have you ever had a moment in life where something comes out of your mouth you didn't even know you were saying until it was too late? Yeah, Holy Spirit will use your own mouth to talk to you sometimes. I responded to my brother, "Well, even if I am going to die, I'm going to do what He told me to do."

This began the journey of going to the places where "no one else wants to go." The very prayer I had asked God. He took my ignorant prayers seriously, because He knows us better than we know ourselves. When we trust Him and follow His leading, He finds a way to make us fall in love with people, places, and things that seem so far out of our comfort zone, even in war zones.

One of God's main priorities in our lives is building a relationship with us built on trust. A relationship where we are dependent on Him. The type of relationship where there is absolutely nothing He could ask of us that we wouldn't say yes to. He's looking for believers totally yielded to Him and this only comes through trust.

It wasn't until I was lying in my bed in Democratic Republic of Congo listening to the gun shots come closer and closer that I ever questioned if just His word to go would be enough.

2

SEASON OF BLISS

I CAN STILL REMEMBER THE VERY FIRST TIME I STEPPED ON THE ground in DRC. I was going to work with an incredible organization that builds schools in war zones. The world called this place the "heart of darkness." It was known as the rape capital of the world. War had been raging for over two decades. There were multiple rebel groups all contending with each other and the government for power. Villages were pillaged by soldiers to steal their crops for nourishment, their boys for battle, and their young girls for brides. This place was an absolute mess. There did not seem to be much hope in the global community that this nation would ever recover; even the majority of the locals seemed to accept war as their fate, but this organization had hope for change.

We stayed with heroic pastors in Goma, the border city with Rwanda. While most non-profits stayed close to the border tucked behind high walls and armed guards, this organization stayed out with the people. It was a journey of zig zagging off the main road through the mamas selling vegetables and charcoal at the street market to make it to our home. The pastors used to live in what is now their kitchen before they were able to expand and add another floor. A simple home made of concrete bricks, we lived on the second story while our pastor and his family lived on the bottom floor. At the time, the house had no electricity or running water. Occasionally, we would spend a little extra money for petrol to run a generator to charge our devices in the one outlet upstairs that worked. Everyone bucket-showered in a tub that was too close to the toilet for my comfort, and because there was no running water, we flushed the toilet with a pitcher of water. The water was retrieved from a massive red trash can that sat just beneath the window, where we had an open view to see down the street. I never could stop thinking that if we could see out, surely others could see in. I tried not to think about it.

Goma had experienced a volcanic eruption and the majority of the city still carried the residue of ash. This meant that by the end of the day, your feet were black and my blonde hair was, well, a color not found in the Guess Who game. It took approximately three washes with cold bucket water before the trace of ash was gone. We tried our best to keep things sanitary, but really? If I ever had moments where I longed for home while I was there, it was standing in the tub, stark naked, holding a pitcher, shaking from the cold, praying no one could see me through the window and dreaming of a hot running shower that would actually make me feel clean. Even as I sit here laughing at the craziness, I feel the ache of missing it. I had fallen in love with the nations and Congo quickly rooted itself deep in my heart. Other than the bathroom, I was living the dream.

If you looked through the window during the day, you could see out over the neighborhood and watch the hustle and bustle amongst the beauty of people and nature. As darkness fell, every person on the street quickly went into their homes. No one stayed out at night, especially us; it was just too risky. Some nights through the window, you could actually see the glow from the active volcano. And on nights of violence, that same window showed the flashing lights of gunfire that lit up our house like the 4th of July.

We cooked in a little room on the side of our living area over a charcoal fire that we built ourselves. We would create a little reservoir in a plastic bag that we would fill with gasoline, then take the little pouch of gasoline and hide it under the coals to get the fire going. Spare your lectures on our health, I've heard them all. You do what you gotta do on the mission field. The job of fanning the coals was a shared job as we gathered as a team each night to eat with either a candle or a headlamp for light. We took turns with most duties because almost anything felt like a chore after a long day. This occasionally meant that we resigned to a protein bar for dinner to avoid extra work. You know you're tired when you'd rather rest than eat.

After dinner was finished, every dish would be washed by hand in two buckets that we left in the room we cooked in, another reason for the protein bars. I never minded washing the dishes or starting the fire, but I hated being the one who had to walk downstairs to go outside in the dark and empty the washing buckets. It was necessary though, because if you left the water in them too long, the stench was awful. We would put water on the fire each night to pour into the canteens so that we could have a hot cup of tea.

Each morning, we woke up to hopefully have enough hot water in the canteens left over from the night before. Usually breakfast was a banana and nuts, or if we really felt like splurging, we would hop across the alley to our neighbor who made the

Congolese version of a doughnut, called a mendazi. These were a slice of heaven with a cup of hot tea before we headed out for the day.

Most days, we would walk to the school or hop on a motorbike. Honestly, I still do not know which was more eventful or even dangerous. The walk was long and followed by stares from every direction, often with children screaming out "Mizungu" or "white person" and waving frantically. I did not mind the walk, but you never knew when a calm situation could turn into chaos. Desperate people will do desperate things to survive, and this culture had been in survival mode for far too long.

The motorbike taxis, on the other hand, drove like they were qualifying for NASCAR. They disregarded all traffic laws and occasionally tried to slip a hand on your knee while you were sitting behind them. This, of course, always merited a strong "HAPANA" or "NO" in Swahili, which they followed with roaring laughter. Despite multiple awkward situations on the back of a motorbike, it was one of my favorite things. I could sit there with the wind blowing in my face and enjoy the views of daily life. We would pass mamas carrying heavy loads on their heads and men huddled up playing cards, children playing soccer with tied up plastic bags or walking to school with backpacks that were twice the size of their little bodies. I loved these moments of soaking in the culture with not a care in the world, except for when I was fiercely interceding for my life from the carelessness of a crazy driver.

Nothing in Congo necessarily came easy, but it was fulfilling. I was exactly where I wanted to be, but more importantly, I had the distinct knowing of being exactly where He wanted me to be.

3

GUNSHOTS RANG OUT

I DON'T ACTUALLY REMEMBER HOW LONG INTO THE TRIP WE HAD BEEN there when the gunshots first rang out at night. War was common in the village, and for that reason, we spent most of our time in the city taking occasional trips to visit the village. In the city, we were not typically as concerned about the threat of war or extreme violence. A few gun shots here or there was nothing to be alarmed by. It could be a neighbor trying to warn off thieves or perhaps a drunk soldier who had lost his temper. This time, though, the shots did not stop for over an hour.

I was no stranger to bullets flying. Neither was the team. Yet this time, something felt eerily different. As the shooting drew closer, a feeling came that I had not felt in a long time. It was fear. It's kind of crazy what you can normalize if you're around it enough. That night, though, I lay in bed and the fear grew until it was paralyzing. As I lay there, His familiar voice came: "Jessika, if you can't trust Me in moments like this, then I can't trust you in places like this."

I immediately knew this was another monumental "I set before you life and death" moment. He made a statement and it demanded a response. I would either give into my fear in the midst of actual present danger or I would trust Him. I knew this decision was bigger than just this one occasion. I knew that trusting Him here would have a lasting effect on me. My brain and heart were racing. The gunshots were close. What happens if the men make it into the house? You really don't want to think about it, but how do you not? I sat with His statement. I thought about our history. I knew I had to make a decision. I whispered to Him, "I trust you," and the fear immediately lifted. Lying there in that bed, the threat of death was very real. But Perfect Love cast out my fear.

The gun shots became a nighty occurrence, and so much of the next few weeks were now a blur. We would lay in our beds and hear our neighbors crying out for help. There are not words to accurately explain what that felt like, to travel to another country with a burning desire to help and love its people, only to have to lie there and listen to their screams with no way to intervene. It was gut wrenching.

There were several times the shooters came right to our house. One night in particular, a man stood outside our gate blowing a horn to signal for his friends to come join him. We lay in our beds listening to him blow the horn over and over again. The horn was like those you take to a soccer game to cheer for your team. To this day, I still cannot stand to hear that sound without having a nauseating feeling sit in my stomach.

Night after night, we heard them make their way up our street, house by house. We would each lay in our own bed, awake, praying. It got to the point where we would dread the night. After dinner, we would stay up watching downloaded shows on our laptops attempting to escape the chaos that was undoubtedly coming. I would put my headphones in as I climbed into bed, hoping that even if there was shooting, perhaps I could turn my worship music up loud enough and just sleep right through it. That rarely worked, but it brought a sense of peace in the chaos.

We were absolutely exhausted, trying to sleep amidst gunfire at night, then still going out to do what needed to be done during the day. Rumors were going around about what was really happening, but no one really knew. Was it bandits? Rebels? Government soldiers? Was it going to stop any time soon? Were they targeting us, the only white foreigners in the neighborhood? Should we leave? Should we stay? If we stay, were we putting our hosts, whom we love, in danger? If we leave, were we abandoning them when they needed us the most? Will they eventually get into our house? What will happen then? We all knew what was possible and we found it easiest to pretend it wasn't really happening.

One day, we were at the school and the administrator was acting differently. He had us sit in the office where he began to tell my friend a story in Swahili. He had tears in his eyes and so did she. I could tell something horrible had happened. We soon found out that one of the students of the school had been brutally murdered by witch doctors. We had distributed the Samaritan's Purse Christmas boxes and spent the afternoon laughing as the students received their gifts with so much excitement just a few days before. This little boy in particular was over-the-top thrilled. That afternoon as he walked home from school, he was taken, abused, and killed.

So many thoughts ran through my head in that moment. The "what if's" were brutal. What if we would have stayed longer? What if we would have walked him home? Did we miss something? Was Holy Spirit speaking and we did not hear Him? Why did this young boy have to die on our watch?

We were all shaken. We were all hurting. We went home and did what we knew best: we prayed and we worshipped. Death seemed to be hovering around us like a cloud.

After one crazy night of shooting, my sweet friend walked out of the room and looked at me. Her face was weary and all she said was, "I am so tired of war." As I sit here writing this, years later, I remember that moment so clearly. She finally voiced what we all had been feeling. God had been showing up mightily in so many ways of protection and miracles, but the weeks of little sleep, horrifying stories, and constant threat of rape or death was getting to us all. We weren't less happy, we were simply tired.

Through all of this, I was not aware of the toll that was being taken on my body, my emotional health, and my faith. In life, we often just do what we have to do. We don't take the time to stop and think about what we're feeling or what might be going on inside of us. We'll talk later about the importance of self awareness, but maybe this is the best time to let you know I was completely unaware of what was really going on inside of me. Over the course of years, I had learned to stuff in my emotions. I had decided that they were unnecessary and problematic. When I felt tired, frustrated, or wanted to complain, I just reminded myself of how much worse others had it. In my opinion at the time, these emotions did more harm than good, and the best thing I could do was learn to ignore them. For someone who never wanted to be martyred, I had a severe martyr complex. I had no idea how much trouble this would make for me in my future.

One afternoon, we were taking motorbike taxis back home when a downpour hit. We stopped at one of our favorite little local restaurants to wait out the storm, as fast drivers and muddy roads are a bad combination. This particular restaurant was a hidden gem. Frequented by United Nations peacekeepers and NGO workers, it was like an oasis in a desert for us. The restaurant is situated right on the lake with beautiful green grass, lounge chairs overlooking the water, horrible instant coffee, and a decent Caesar salad. The best part of all: no guns allowed. Here we could actually pretend that we were on vacation on some exotic tropical island, or I tried to. We loved to come on the weekends to escape and use the painfully slow Wifi. This time, we were sitting out on the patio and waiting for our food when a loud BOOM came from somewhere way too close. We instinctively hit the deck below our table, fearing that violence had invaded our oasis. We soon realized that lightning had struck about hundred meters from us on the lake. The waiters laughed at us as we tried to gracefully recoup. This was when I first realized that maybe, just maybe, I was just a little on edge. Everything and everyone was starting to feel like a threat. This is not a healthy mental state.

About this time, my friend got a word from the Lord. He told her that in battle, He sends the musicians out in front, and it was time we started worshipping every night before bed. So we did. That first night, we sat there all absolutely exhausted and we sang to Him. We worshipped Him. We cried. Then we went to bed. There was not a single gunshot that night.

It continued. Night after night, exhausted, we would still gather to worship. Admittedly, several nights I fell asleep on that couch fighting to muster the energy, but our hearts were locked in. We did not worship to stop war. We worshipped because He was worthy in the midst of war. In the midst of pain. In the midst of our heartache. And night after night, there were no gunshots after we worshipped.

One night, we came in after a particularly hard day and we

decided we would just go to bed that night. That was the first night that the gun shots came back. We all learned a valuable lesson that day. <u>Worship is warfare</u>. We did not carry knives or guns, we were surrounded by bombs, helicopters, and weapons, but our worship was our warfare.

When the time came to go home, we were all ready. We all knew in our hearts we needed a break, but we would all be coming back... or so I thought. Little did I know what was waiting for me back home.

4

TRIBULATIONS COME

"In this life you will have tribulation; but take heart, I have overcome the world." —Jesus

THIS IS NOT THE VERSE WE LIKE TO PUT ON A REFRIGERATOR MAGNET. The guarantee of trials from the Man Himself. I don't think I've ever seen a bumper sticker that says, "Honk if you love trials!" I'm a proponent of focusing on things that bring hope and, of course, being well-versed in the promises of the Word, but we cannot assume that following Christ means life will be easy.

In my younger years, I was somehow convinced that as long as I loved Him and I obeyed Him, things would never be "too hard." No one told me this per se, this is just the notion I picked up along the way. Most have heard the phrase, "God will not give you more than you can bear," and I used this to create the belief I would never feel like life was more than I can bear. I thought that my devotion to Him was complemented by His unending protection of my happiness. At its best, this belief results in a self-centered

Gospel that never ventures out of my comfort zone, and at its worst, it leaves me broken and confused, unable to reconcile the god of my mind and the True God of the Bible.

When we take on a theological perspective that exempts us from suffering or sacrifice, we are cutting out a large portion of Scripture to pacify ourselves while simultaneously cultivating an expectation that is altogether unrealistic. So many Christians try to pretend like everything in life is always going to go well that it is no wonder the world has a hard time taking us seriously. Some of us can be looking trauma right in the face and trying to pretend like it isn't real or doesn't cause us pain. We beckon to a lost world, "Come and follow Jesus, then everything in your life will be better." This straight up isn't what Jesus said. He said there would be difficulty, opposition, and persecution, but with every adversity, there are promises that accompany it.

I like Mother Theresa's quote: "I know God won't give me more than I can handle, I just wished He didn't trust me so much." We have to stop thinking that God has a goal of preventing all challenges in our lives and start seeing the True God who, in fact, uses challenges for His ultimate goal. There are a number of reasons we could be dealing with hard times. It could be we are experiencing an attack from the devourer who delights in our pain. Perhaps we're going through a time of pruning and testing by God Himself. Maybe we're just experiencing the consequences of our own actions or simply the brokenness of living in a fallen world with broken people. No matter the origination of our trouble, God never stops being faithful. This is our anchor. This is our hope.

"You called out to Me in your time of trouble and I rescued you. I came down from the realm of the secret place of thunder, where mysteries hide. I came down to save you. I tested your hearts at the place where there was no water to drink, the place of your bitter argument with me." (Psalm 81:7 TPT)

In Hebrew, the word used to describe the place where the Israelites were is Maribeh. This word literally means "the place of strife and contention" (Brian Simmons, footnotes). He tests our hearts in the place of strife and contention. This is sobering.

If we are honest with ourselves, all too often when we are in our Maribeh places, what comes out of our hearts is not pretty. We can become introspective, full of shame and guilt, or even accusatory, trying to find a way to blame other people for our pain. We can be selfish. In Maribeh, a mirror is held up for us to see things in our hearts we often do not know are there until circumstances reveal it. A true look into who we really are is necessary, and often it takes those adverse circumstances for the hidden attributes in our heart to come to the surface.

We cannot ignore the fact that if God allows us to be in a place of strife and contention, there must be something for us there. Is it possible that a good God uses our pain, or perhaps He even leads us into painful tests? I know, this messed with my theology, too. All too often, I find those who struggle the most with tribulation are the ones that think God's goodness somehow prevents hardship. Our false expectation of who He is sets us up for greater disappointment. It causes us to miss divine opportunities for increase. Our hope can not be placed in the avoidance of trials, but rather in the nature of God in our trials.

In Luke chapter five, there is a story about a man who has leprosy. Jesus was coming through town and the man cries out to Him: "Lord if you are willing, you can make me clean" (Luke 5:12).

The man was taking a big risk calling out to Jesus like this. At the time, the belief was that if you had leprosy, then you had sinned. It was your own fault if you had this horrible, flesh-eating disease. You were sentenced to being "unclean," and you would have had no right to approach Jesus and make such a request of Him. In the man's desperation, he cries out to Jesus for healing.

Notice that he does not say, "God, if you can, please heal me." Instead, he says, "If you are willing, you can..." This man did not doubt Jesus' ability, but he was, however, unsure of His nature. He knew that Jesus had the ability to heal, but He was not convinced that He would be willing to heal him, the leprous sinner. Hebrews 1:3 says that Jesus is the exact imprint of God's nature. Jesus' response to this man declares the nature of God: "I am willing, be clean."

When trials come, we usually do not doubt God's *ability* to help us. We doubt His *willingness*, we doubt His nature. We must be convinced of God's nature, especially in adversity. We must look to the Word for who He says He is.

The enemy wants you to doubt God's nature, and ultimately, he wants you to quit. It's his purpose for your trial. However, God has a purpose for your trial, too. God desires for this trial to solidify His nature in you and propel you further forward. Every single trial in life comes with an invitation to know God at a deeper level than you knew Him before.

When we believe God is most concerned about our life being easy, we will miss the invitation hidden in our trials. Look at this passage in Psalms:

> "How enriched are they who find their strength in the Lord; within their hearts are the highways of holiness! Even when their paths wind through the dark valley of tears, they dig deep to find a pleasant pool where others find only pain. He gives to them a brook of blessing filled from the rain of an outpouring.

They grow stronger and stronger with every step forward, and the God of all gods will appear before them in Zion." (Psalm 84:5-7 TPT)

In the valley of tears, some people will only find pain, yet others will see the brook of blessing. Both types of people experience the tears. Both are in the valley. Some see opportunity for increase and others only see loss. Which type of person will you be?

Jesus loves you. His love, shown to us on the cross, is beyond comprehension and beyond explanation. The hang up to what we see is not His love, but our self-defined version of love.

His testing, His allowing of trials, are not in contradiction to love. He is abundantly good. He is extravagantly kind. One of my favorite verses says that He delights in the welfare of his servants (Psalm 35:27). And yet He is still a God who intentionally orchestrates our discomfort for His glory and our benefit. He is still a God that does not immediately rescue us from every hard situation. He is still a God that tells us that we have an enemy that roams around seeking someone to devour.

My friends, tribulations will come. Our triumph is not found in never seeing battle. It is found in Christ who has overcome the world. It is in trusting that God will work all things, including our painful seasons, tests, and trials, for our good (Romans 8:28).

This is my prayer, found in Psalm 86:

"Teach me more about you, how you work and how you move, so that I can walk onward in your truth until everything within me brings honor to your name" (Psalm 86:11 TPT)

5

THE FORGOTTEN RANCH

WHEN I RETURNED TO TEXAS, I TRULY THOUGHT I WAS THE HAPPIEST I had ever been. I left Congo alive and inspired. I was already planning my next trip back. In Texas, I was running an organization I adored and doing projects in nations I had only dreamed of. I was working with a church that was like family to me. I had no idea that my life was about to get totally flipped upside down.

About a week after being home, I first heard the screams. I woke up panicked, covered in sweat. Where were the shooters? Who was being hurt? Where was I? I was having a nightmare, but this was not abnormal after a trip into a war zone. More often than not, I came home with a head full of brutal war stories, completely unaware of how to process them with those around me. The life of guns and machetes I left behind was too foreign to the world of prosperity surrounding me upon my return.

I stepped into the shower and turned the water all the way to the hottest possible temperature. My place of rescue and peace. As the water flowed down, I noticed there was no ash to wash out, and I burst into tears. Far away, my friends were still there washing with a bucket of cold water. How come I had hot running water and they had bullets? Were they just victims of geography and me the recipient of privilege? Unprocessed emotions that had been buried for years were boiling under the surface, coming dangerously close to the front. Questions that I didn't think I was allowed to ask were begging for resolution.

I had been home about a week when my mom went and bought a meal I had been craving from a local restaurant. A perfect burger and fries with the best ranch dressing ever created. She was so excited to do this for me because she knew how much I loved it. When she brought the food in to the house for dinner, I quickly realized the worst possible thing: she had forgotten the most important part of the meal: the ranch dressing. All my Texans say, *Amen.* I began unpacking the bag, eagerly looking for my dressing. After each bag was empty, the realization hit me, there was no ranch and my blood began to boil. I sat there eating each fry without my ranch. With each bite, I became increasingly upset. Every single fry was a reminder that I didn't have that dressing, the object of my affection. I was trying so hard to keep my emotions in. I knew in my brain that this was absolutely ridiculous, yet I could not seem to get my feelings under control. After a few minutes, it caused me so much frustration that I just lost control and cried. What a beautiful picture... war zone missionary cries over forgotten ranch dressing!

Thankfully, the french fry debacle is now a funny family memory. At the time, it was the first indicator that something wasn't quite right, however, I chose to ignore the warning sign and press on.

I was low on patience with very little compassion for those around me or myself. In the moment, all of my responses seemed logical. Part of this is just the reality of post traumatic stress disorder that I wasn't even aware of yet, but a large part was due to the fact that I had been shoving emotions down for years. I wish I could blame everything that unravels in the coming chapters on the PTSD, but the truth was, I had many areas of weakness that were about to be exposed. In my attempts to have strong faith, I avoided all of my doubts, my frustrations, my negative emotions—everything that seemed to negate my "beliefs." I didn't want to face the evident contradictions with the God of my faith and the world of war. I had worn a mask for so long that I had lost all true self-awareness.

After just a few weeks into this ordeal, I had a trip planned with a friend out to my alma mater. It had been years since I had made it back to Lubbock, Texas, home of Texas Tech University (Wreck 'em), and I was so excited when we first started planning the trip. However, as the trip got closer I became nervous. My nightmares had only intensified, when in the past, they usually began to fade after a week or two. I knew I was agitated, although I was having a hard time pinpointing the source of my frustrations.

This friend and I were very close, and she'd hinted more than once that while in town, I should take the opportunity to sit down with one of my favorite professors, who happened to be a licensed professional counselor. I had every intention of visiting my professor and zero intention of telling her the truth about my condition. A few times while in Congo, I had emailed her to discuss some of the brutality and tragedy, mostly to ask for advice on activities we could do that would help the victims we met with, and also to connect to someone I knew could stomach the more gruesome details.

When we arrived at her house, the visit started out normal, but I soon realized neither my friend nor my professor were going to let me leave without me opening up. It took a little bit of prying and then I tried to talk, but the tears came first. No one had asked me about specifics because no one really knew them, except my professor, and we both knew that she knew. Tears just streamed slowly down my face and I never could really formulate the words to describe what was going on. Before we left, my professor asked one thing of me: talk to someone and do it soon. She gave me one week.

I had hoped walking out her door would put an end to these subtle hints people were giving me about therapy, but that was far from reality. My friend and I had multiple conflicts on the remainder of the trip, and after a few more outbursts with others, I had enough people pleading with me to see a therapist that I obliged. The truth is, I felt shame just at the suggestion that I needed it. Years of studying counseling in college, championing others to do it, and yet here I was, still feeling the weight of condemnation because people thought I needed it. It felt like an attack on my strength, on my identity, on my ability to manage my own life. I decided to give the therapist a call, get the okay that I was fine, and prove to everyone that they were overly concerned— that they were just plain wrong. I was fine. I would get through this on my own like I always had.

After a fifteen minute phone interview, the therapist said I clearly had PTSD and needed to come in for sessions. In the meantime, she wanted to prescribe me an antidepressant, an anti-anxiety med, and a sleep aid. I hung up the phone thinking that shrink had lost her mind. I don't remember the details of the interview, but I do remember thinking I was crushing it. I'm sure with no shock to you at all, I disregarded the therapist's recommendation and decided even if something was wrong, Jesus would heal me of it. I was a strong woman of faith, after all.

6

THE GIFT OF PAIN

WHEN I WAS FIFTEEN YEARS OLD, I HAD A SEVERE SHOULDER INJURY playing softball that needed to have a fairly extensive surgery to correct. While waiting for the surgery date, the doctors had me on high doses of painkillers to try and keep me comfortable. I would take two pills every four hours and often could barely feel a thing. Even though the pain was gone, my shoulder was unable to function properly. In fact, the doctors told me that every move I made needed to be with my shoulder in mind. I shouldn't pick up any weight, because even if I didn't feel the pain, lifting even a minuscule amount could hurt me even more. I was unable to do most of my simple normal activities, including dressing and showering.

After the surgery, I was put in a sling and had a morphine pump that was put directly into my shoulder. Whenever the pain came, I simply pressed a button and morphine was immediately injected right into the site of the pain. This was a straight up gift from heaven. A kiss that wiped away the pain. There was not one single time I considered not pushing that button when I felt pain.

It would be absurd to have the power to immediately alleviate my pain and choose not to. Right?

This reminds me of how our society views pain and the process of pain in our lives. We do whatever is necessary to alleviate pain immediately without considering the long term consequences of those actions. If I would have assumed my shoulder was fixed simply because I felt no pain, then I would have not only failed at trying to use it as normal, but also would have caused more damage. Many people use self-medicating techniques to alleviate their pain, but they're doing nothing to fix the actual root problems in their character and circumstances. Embracing pain and brokenness invites us into the beauty of God's complete healing and redemption.

If we attempt to alleviate pain before we've allowed God to work in us or in our situation, we might begin to think we're healed, when in reality, we're not living life to our full capacity. Just like with my shoulder, we begin to live adjusted to our brokenness, never achieving all that we could do if we were fully healed. We normalize our dysfunction and call it wholeness. I could have spent the rest of my life using painkillers to alleviate the pain in my shoulder, never being able to use it for what it was created for.

This is where pain becomes beneficial. Pain is actually an indicator. Pain points you in the direction of your true condition and is often used by Holy Spirit to reveal your true condition TO YOU. Pain is not the problem; it *points* us toward the problem. Without pain, we would continue on, oblivious to the real issues in our hearts and lives. Let's be honest: we as a generation aren't that great at being aware of the source of our pain. We have created distractions to keep us from having to deal with our true condition.

Self awareness is actually so vital in life. We should be aware of what is going on inside of us. Many times, our pain will uncover deep rooted issues that have been buried for years, or sometimes it simply shows a recently developing sin pattern that the enemy is trying to ensnare us with. Pain is even used by God to snap us out of a place of complacency. Either way, pain can become dangerous when ignored, just like a wound can become infected when left untreated. My prayer is that even now while reading this book, Holy Spirit is highlighting areas of pain in your life. He's giving you insight to understand why you have pain around certain memories, topics, or even people.

When we aren't self aware, we ignorantly allow our fear of pain to be what directs our steps instead of the One we claim to follow. There are many people who are making pain the Lord of their lives by allowing pain to determine their actions. Little do they know that their determination to avoid pain is actually causing them to miss out on some of the greatest gifts Jesus has to offer. Their pain tells them to avoid certain circumstances or even certain people. Let's get real. We've all been there. Jenny Sue made a comment that pricked me. I didn't ask her what she meant by it. I didn't take it before Jesus. I let it fester and fester until soon I found myself totally avoiding Jenny. Jenny is unsafe, I tell myself. Jenny is critical. Jenny has the potential to be "toxic," so I should probably set a boundary to protect myself from her. Soon, I'm believing all sorts of lies about Jenny, not because of Jenny, but because of my own pain. There is so much to be said about the culture right now that says to "cancel" the toxic people in our lives. More often than not, we label people as toxic so that we don't have to deal with our own dysfunction.

In these scenarios, I'm avoiding any situation that might cause me pain and, of course, calling myself wise in the process. The truth is, I'm scared. When we're not self aware, we will allow our fear of pain to guide us and think we're choosing wisdom. I never stopped to ask why Jenny's comment pricked me. I was totally unaware that there was an unhealed wound in my life that Jenny unintentionally rubbed up against. Imagine how differently this scenario plays out if I see that pain as an indicator. Jenny isn't my enemy. Jenny just helped me realize that I need to go to Jesus to deal with an unresolved wound. I immediately forgive Jenny and use this situation for further healing, or at the very least, I go to Jenny and give her the opportunity to communicate her intentions. Jenny and I remain friends. Imagine that. Maybe Jenny isn't toxic, perhaps I just didn't know how to process what caused me pain.

One of the best examples of being self aware was King David. We see a great picture confirming this in the Psalms when David says, "Why are you downcast oh my soul?" He noticed the pain in his heart and he went toward it instead of away from it. He asked himself the questions many of us never take the time to do. Instead of running from the depression in his heart, he labeled it and sought solutions.

David did not randomly ask his soul why it was downcast. He clearly was self aware enough to recognize that it was downcast! That means he was very aware of what was going on inside of him and leaned in to discover what steps to take. Yeah, it's easier in the moment to deny what is really going on. It strokes our pride to think we're just really great at managing ourselves. The years you're going to spend cleaning up the messes you make because of your avoidance aren't worth it, though. Trust me.

Self awareness plays a major role not only in healing, but in living life fully, whole hearted, and aware of the attacks of the enemy. People who aren't self aware are susceptible to many lies from the enemy. When I was going through PTSD, I began to believe crazy lies about myself. In fact, at one point, I even believed I might be demon possessed! I thought everyone was rejecting me. I thought that no one wanted me around. I truly believed that I was going to die. I began to think that everyone around me could sense my lack of self worth and they thought that I was as big of a failure as I had begun to believe about myself. I was so out of touch with who I was that I was susceptible to multiple lies from the enemy. It was ruining my perception of myself and others. Instead of searching for the root of these thoughts and emotions, I simply accepted them as truth.

Have you ever had those thoughts that caused you to question your salvation? The thoughts that questioned your significance? How about the thoughts that say that no one cares about you and you're all alone in this world? As I've traveled and shared this message, I've heard countless stories of people who have heard and believed the exact same lies I did. The enemy is not extremely creative. He's been using the same lies and the same deception for centuries.

What if we stopped running from our pain, and instead, learned to turn and face it? What if we grew aware of what is going on inside ourselves and then we took our masks off to address it?

It is fascinating that Jesus came to bind up all of our wounds, and yet we try to hide from them. The Word actually says God is near the broken hearted, which means He is very aware we will have moments of deep heartache. Even greater than that, He doesn't hide from us in these moments. He comes near.

Many times, it is actually a gift of God when your inner world begins to show on the outside, because it takes coming face to face with your true self in order to see your desperate need for Him. God's disclosure of us to us is an act of mercy. He will repeatedly speak to us about us. He will give us warning signs. He will try to reveal our areas of weakness to us first, perhaps to close community, but when we don't listen, eventually, it will be exposed. As the Word says, what has been in the dark will come to light. It is not a matter of if, but when.

7

CHURCH MASKS

THE NIGHTMARES OFTEN CONSISTED OF MEN WITH GUNS CHARGING into my house. I would hear them right outside blowing the horns they used in Congo. I could hear the invaders' feet near my window. Even when I woke up, I couldn't seem to convince myself that no one was trying to rape or kill me. This had been going on for over a month, and by this time, I had stopped being able to sleep at all. If I was able to get an hour or two combined, then it was a good night.

I was working in my local church and I had a routine where I would go early to get into the sanctuary and pray before everyone made their way in for the work day. I was setting my bags down at my desk and gathering my things to take to prayer one day when I heard it. Pop! Pop! Pop! Someone was outside. I heard whispering. Were they surrounding the building? Wait. Calm down. I'm in Liberty, Texas, for goodness sake. But... I heard it. They were shuffling outside the door. Maybe they wanted to rob the church and they saw me go in by myself. No. I'm in Texas. No one is there. But the fear came. My arms went numb.

I climbed under my desk and began to cry. I knew that I was in Texas. I knew that men were not strolling up to the church with AK-47s. Why didn't my brain know what I knew? It felt as though I was losing my mind. Hallucinations like this became common.

At night, if I stayed in bed, I would toss and turn hearing voices, seeing demons, sweating, and crying all night. I would pull my head out from under my covers to see red eyes moving in my room. Multiple nights, I would "wake up" to find myself in the front yard looking through the bushes for the baby I heard crying in my mind or the neighbor I thought had been shot. Occasionally, I would have a moment where I would realize that what I was doing was irrational. But those moments would thrust me further into despair, believing the lie I needed to be institutionalized. Ironically, when you start believing that you're crazy, it seems to speed up the process.

At first, I did my best to do the spiritual thing. I would rebuke the fear, the demon, the whatever I could think of, telling it to leave in the name of Jesus over and over again. I would pray in tongues. I would quote Scripture. But my symptoms didn't stop. Eventually, I stopped believing I had the power to do anything and would resort to just pulling the covers over my head while waiting miserably until morning.

I spent the majority of my energy trying to prevent a trigger that would no doubt thrust me into a pit of despair I did not know how to escape. The worst part was that I went into these pits alone. I wouldn't allow anyone to see my reality.

One night, my spiritual mom followed me home from church in her car. She was most likely coming to check on me as she happened to be on the receiving end of the worst parts of my breakdown. I kept seeing her car in the rear view mirror and terror was sweeping my brain. I was thinking that she wanted to hurt me. I did not know why, I just remember feeling like I needed to protect myself from her. Often I would "know" something was not true, but I could not convince my body of it. I knew she did not want to hurt me. I knew she only wanted to help. My brain, however, thought she was a threat. I remember this moment so vividly because I wanted to tell her what I was feeling. I wanted to tell her what my brain was saying to me, but I thought if I told her, she would think I was crazy. I was convinced I was losing my mind and did not know if I would ever get it back.

The anxiety eventually became so bad that it was hard to eat. Panic attacks came where I felt like I was having a heart attack or psychotic breakdown. My chest would hurt or my arm would go numb. With my body quickly losing energy from lack of sleep and nutrition, I found myself totally unable to exercise. I would put on my running shoes and drive to the local park, only to have a panic attack as soon as I stepped out onto the trail.

I started having suicidal thoughts. At first, just a few a day while I was driving down the road in my car. I would think, *Just drive into a tree; someone will think you fell asleep. Maybe they will think you checked your phone and lost control. No one has to know that you chose to end your life.* The 'just a few a day' thoughts grew to hundreds a day. It was no longer driven by making it an accident; instead, it was just the overwhelming desire to end all of the pain. I considered buying a gun to shoot myself or downing some toxic substance.

During all of this, I had to lead a short-term team to Haiti. Let me stop and give one piece of advice: if you're having a total and complete mental breakdown while entertaining suicidal thoughts, consider NOT leading teams on mission to other countries.

I had been trying very hard to hide how I was really doing. I thought as a leader, it was my job to be okay. We could say I faked it, but if we're being honest, I just lied a lot. I lied to everyone around me hoping they would not know I was crumbling to pieces and barely hanging on for life.

A few days before we were set to leave, I went to my pastor and, through tears, told him I could not do it. I had no idea how I was going to get on a plane and leave the country, much less how I would find the capacity to lead a team. This rare moment of honesty was brief, but then I was deeply ashamed at my vulnerability. My pastor told me that if I could not lead the trip, then he would take the team for me. His offer of help felt like an insult, so I recanted the next day. When it was time to go, my main step of preparation was putting on a mask that I could do this just fine.

We landed in Haiti, and just getting off the plane was sending my anxiety through the roof. I was fighting every single moment not to thrust head-on into an uncontrollable panic attack. The anxiety was unbearable. I do not know what would have happened if I did not have one of my best friends on the trip. I had no choice but to be honest with her, since she knew what I was going through, so she joined the fight to keep me from having a total mental collapse.

As soon as we left the airport after arriving, the missionary took us to a restaurant that had a man standing outside on guard with a rifle. One look at the gun sent me into a spin. I walked to the side of the restaurant trying not to collapse on the floor. My friend followed me over and just began to comfort me and talk me into peace. I gripped on to a table, tears filling my eyes, anxiety ripping through my body. I took slow breaths. I begged God to just help me keep it together. Most of my "prayers" in this season were basically begging and bargaining to keep me from dying or having others find out how sick I was. After a few minutes, I was able to get myself under control and I walked back to my team, mask in place, pretending everything was fine. Throughout the trip, I would walk onto the roof of the house where we were staying and contemplate jumping off the side to end all my pain.

One of these times I was so desperate, I threw open my Bible in frustration and began to read. I was searching for an answer. For healing. For anything to get me out of this proverbial hell. It felt like a verse was jumping off the page at me: "May the God of hope fill you with peace and joy as you trust in Him, so that you may abound in hope" (Romans 15:13). I burst into tears. I had no hope, no peace, no joy, and I was struggling desperately to trust Him in the lowest, most painful season of my life. Would this God of hope whom I had served for so long come and fill me with peace and joy? I was struggling to believe it, but I wanted to. When we returned home from Haiti, I wrote that verse on note cards and put them everywhere to read. I would quote it daily through tears, trying to make myself believe there was still hope for me.

This was not a season of deep heartache accompanied by His overwhelmingly felt Presence. He was there, I see that so clearly now, but I couldn't feel Him or hear Him while consumed by my trials. God only seemed to interrupt in the moments when I was about to end it all and I just didn't understand. He promises that He is near the brokenhearted. He did not feel near. But there I was in ministry with my mask firmly in place telling people He was.

I was losing everything, and the harder I fought to maintain it, the faster it was slipping through my fingers. Slowly, I was losing the ability to hide my condition from those around me. That meant I was about to lose something I did not even realize was so precious to me: my reputation. My reputation for being strong and brave. My reputation of having it all together, all the time. People were about to find out what God had always knownI was human. Perhaps they knew, and I was the one who didn't.

We cannot allow the fear of losing reputation keep us from taking the journey of complete healing. Reputation must be left at the cross if we are to become who God has called us to be. My self-imposed religious reputation I had built in small-town Texas was enough to make me try with all my might to hide behind a mask of false security. Honestly, it's comical now when I think about what I thought I had to protect. Your reputation isn't worth jeopardizing the condition of your heart for decades to come. It's certainly not worth continuing to abuse the ones you love and are meant to minister to. Mostly, it is not worth hiding yourself from the One who gave His all for you. The real you, right where you are, not who or where you pretend to be.

When we get used to putting on our mask for those around us, we often unconsciously begin to put on a mask for God, as well. Is it possible that it isn't that God is far off in your trial, He just refuses to meet with a mask? He isn't looking for the perfect version of you that you want to project. He wants you. Right where you are right now. No matter how jacked up you may be.

Jesus said, "Come to me all you who are weary and heavy laden and I will give you rest" (Matthew 11:23). Mysteriously, He didn't say, come to Me all who are put together and equipped to change the world. God is a God of authenticity; it's the enemy who loves masks and counterfeits.

Look at these verses:

Let burning coals fall upon them! Let them be cast into fire, into miry pits, no more to rise! (Psalm 140:10)

Let their eyes be darkened so that they cannot see, and make their loins tremble continually. (Psalm 69:22)

Look to the right and see: there is none who takes notice of me; no refuge remains to me; no one cares for my soul. (Psalm 142:4)

When I read these verses, I see a person that is in desperate need of a transformed mind. A man who needs Jesus to come and wash his heart with mercy and identity. Isn't it wild that these words were penned by the man that God says was after His heart? These words are hardly ones that cause a deep respect for the author, this man who slept with another man's wife and then committed murder to cover his own sin. We read the story of David and we often find hope for our own past mistakes and sins. David's life is not even the best example of highest integrity, so what is it that would make him the man after God's heart? What did he possess that God found so desirable? I believe the answer is found in the very verses I began with. Not his temper, his anger, or his shortcomings, but rather his authenticity in the Secret Place. David bore his heart and soul before God. The good, the bad, the horrendous.

If I heard these same prayers from the pulpit on a Sunday morning, I would likely find another church, yet in His Presence, these words seem to attract God. I believe it is because of God's nature to exchange. We see it throughout Scripture: Come to me with your burdens and I'll give you rest. Cast your cares on me and I'll give you peace. Confess your sins and I'll give you forgiveness. In other words, bring what is broken, what is heavy, what is wrong, and I'll exchange it for something better. Here in this place, God is giving us an invitation beyond our wildest imagination: Give Me the ugly things and I'll exchange it for something beautiful. Isaiah

61 depicts it so perfectly when it says He gives beauty for ashes, joy for mourning. With the promise of such a great exchange, what is it that holds us back?

No matter how much I know this Truth, no matter how high a value I have for authenticity, I still find myself trying to put my dirty pieces back together before I go before the Lord. When my heart is still angry toward someone, I tell Him it's not, because surely God will not be happy if I told Him what I was really feeling. That's right. I lie to Him. I catch myself often, rather He points it out, saying what I think He wants me to feel as opposed to what I really feel. I know what I "should" feel, and in light of knowing what should be felt, I hate admitting that I don't. *Oh please, Lord, bless sister so-and-so, I don't mind at all that she treated me like crap. I'm not hurting, I'm not bothered. Can't you see? I'm so much like You, Jesus.* While He's sitting there thinking, *Jess, I know your real heart. I see what you're not saying.* Surely, it cannot be okay to tell God that I want to slap someone or I wished I'd never befriended that person who betrayed me. Am I really allowed to tell God that I feel like He was absent when I needed Him? I mean, who wouldn't want to tell God to destroy the life of the one who hurt them? But we just can't do that, right? I mean... right?

Unless you're David, the man after God's heart. This really comes back to the core of who God is: a relational God who was willing to sacrifice His Son so that we could be near Him. Imagine sending your son to die to have a relationship with humanity and yet people still come into your presence wearing a mask. He isn't interested in a relationship with who you think you should be, but with who you are. He will not meet you where you pretend to be, but where you are. His nature is to exchange and He can't do that when we refuse to bring our real selves to the table.

I get most frustrated when I think I should be over mourning something or someone. The disappointment happened six months ago; how am I supposed to go tell God today that I'm still bothered by it? My heart hurts. Wasn't it supposed to stop hurting by now? The thoughts of condemnation come: If I really believed God healed me, then I wouldn't be sad. If I really trusted God with my future, then I wouldn't be hurting.

Listen, He's not bothered by where you are. I know, I sound like every other woman you've ever heard preach. That broken record saying "come as you are" and yet it's still so stinking hard to believe. I feel you. Really. And yet, it's no less Truth. He wants YOU. The real you. The messy you. The one who gets bothered, sad, frustrated. The one whose expectations weren't met. The one who is still struggling to bless sister so-and-so even though you know it's the right thing to do. He knew who you were when He saved you. He knew who you were when He called you. He still knows today. He sees that mess and He wants you to bring it to Him, so that He can exchange it. You can't do this alone. He is the one who takes the heart of stone and gives you a heart of flesh, BUT you have to bring that stony ugly thing to the altar. I know, because I tried for so long to bring my mask there instead. Guess what? Nothing changed.

8

MADE FOR COMMUNITY

IN MY TRIAL, EVERYTHING I THOUGHT I KNEW ABOUT HIM AND ABOUT myself was shaken. So many lies were coming constantly. I could trust Him when bullets were flying. I could trust Him in near-death experiences. But I did not know how to trust Him in the level of disappointment and pain I was feeling. Through all of it, I spent most of the time lying to God and others with my church mask on, talking about how much I trusted Him while I was absolutely hopeless. God was waiting for the real me to show up.

My inability to face my issues was affecting many of my relationships, especially those closest to me. If I were being totally honest, previous to this season, I never thought relationships were that important. I saw them more as a tool to achieve our purpose in life. However, when life was falling down around me and those relationships became strained, I realized I had a void I'd never felt before. It took losing relationships for me to understand that friendships aren't just "ministry connections."

Let's address this for a minute. It wasn't that I didn't care about people, it wasn't that I didn't have genuine friendships, it was that the most important thing to me was building a ministry. I ignorantly thought that building a ministry through me was what was most important to Jesus. When this is your top priority, you will look at people as a means to serving your vision. You look for people who can contribute to your dream. This type of outlook will undoubtedly become diluted with selfishness. I truly believe it was unintentional and unrecognized, but the majority of the time, I looked at people initially for what they could do and not for who they were. It's painful to admit even now. That was never the type of person I wanted to be and, again, because of my lack of self awareness, I didn't even realize it was who I had become. The Bible says where there is jealousy and selfish ambition, there will be disorder and every vile practice (James 3:16). Where selfish ambition is, disorder and chaos are sure to follow.

Relationships are vital to our lives. When God said that it wasn't good for man to be alone, we often take this to mean that everyone should marry, but what He actually said was that it is not good for man to be *alone*. In other words, we're wired for community. It is not wrong to desire companionship and deep friendships. We actually become the best version of ourselves when we have community where we can be our authentic selves. When we can be vulnerable and honest about who we really are, we let people in to accept us for the real us and not a pretend version of ourselves. There is great joy in being accepted just as you are. This is how God intended it: that we would experience true acceptance for who we are from Him and from community. He designed us to have relationships where we love deeply and are loved deeply. Relationships are meant to be sources of accountability and encouragement that bring us joy and help equip us for our purpose. Relationships are a gift from heaven.

Because God chose to make us relational beings that function best within community, it is a place the enemy will often attack, especially when you're already facing trials. If you look at the lives of many of our Bible heroes, we find that in the midst of great adversity, there was also great relational struggles. We see it in the life of all the great heroes of the faith like Joseph, Abraham, Moses, and on and on. Many times, David states had problems "with his closest friend" in Psalm 55. Even Jesus faced betrayal and denial from those closest to Him. My point is that no one is immune to the pain of relational struggle, and yet we were designed for relationship.

When you go through extreme trial, everything that can be shaken becomes shaken, including your relationships. Even if it was a healthy relationship before, the enemy will try his best to weasel his way in. But if there was anything unhealthy previously in your relationships, it will rise to the top and become exposed. The enemy's intention is always to steal, kill, and destroy in our lives.

The enemy will attempt to destroy relationships by creating disappointment and planting seeds of accusation. We have to be sure that we have healthy expectations of ourselves and others because this is where he will begin. When we're hurting, we want friends around us who are willing to sacrifice for us, and that is perfectly natural. Jesus said there is no greater love than to lay down one's life for his friends (John 15:13). We hope for friends who will pick up the phone or drop by, pray for us, give us wisdom, simply hold us while we cry; in other words, make sacrifices to be there for us. These relationships are invaluable and I'm so thankful for the ones I have. These aren't unrealistic expectations or even foolish desires; however, we must understand that only Jesus can be there for us all the time. Only Jesus can truly meet all of our needs. Community is necessary, but they are not our main Source. It is easy when we are in need to create expectations of others that are actually unrealistic.

Before I went through PTSD, I already had many unrealistic expectations of my closest friend. When I became sick, those expectations just grew. Now years later, I would even say I was codependent. I expected my friend to be there for me all of the time. To treat me as a priority in her life. I honestly believed that this was the epitome of true friendship: I always show up for you when you need it and you always show up for me when I need it. We had done our best to be that for each other for years, and many times, we were actually able to meet those expectations for each other. But when I became sick, this became impossible for her. The truth was, there was absolutely no way she could have been there for me every second that I needed help. The sicker I became, the larger my expectations of her were, which of course, the more my expectations weren't being met, the more I believed the accusations against her from the enemy. The more I believed those accusations, the more I wanted to control her behavior to meet my needs. There were multiple reasons why our friendship struggled deeply during that season, but the biggest root cause can be summed up this way: my expectations. I wanted her to be something that only Jesus could be. Only He could stay with me through all that was coming against me.

We need to be aware of our expectations of others, especially during trials. It is okay to have certain reasonable expectations, but we must make sure they are realistic and that we are communicating those expectations to the person. Many times, our expectations aren't being met because the person doesn't even know they're there or because they're simply impossible for one human to meet. This is why the community aspect is important. In adversity, you can't rely on just one person, you need a community. You need people you can lean on, so when you're feeling at your weakest, if one person isn't available, someone else will be. I'm so thankful for learning this lesson during PTSD. It has helped me since then to have a community of friends to lean on and not just one person. If one relationship is being attacked or someone is simply unavailable, I have been able to lean on multiple others. I have friends who took me into their houses to binge watch shows or go on vacations with their family during hard times; others who Facetimed daily; and some who gave advice, prayed, or just made me laugh. Each friendship played a different, but beautiful role. I had an entire community that rose up to support me in hardship. I wish I would have understood the value of this type of community years ago. It would have saved me and others so much heartache and disappointment.

The enemy loves to take the soil of our disappointment with others and plant seeds to affect our future. If someone isn't meeting your expectations, he will take the opportunity to breed accusations. These accusations can take multiple forms by either accusing the person involved or even trying to accuse you. I find that many people have deep rooted insecurities in their present because of failed relationships in their past. They take on a cloak of rejection, believing they're not worthy to be loved or cared for. This can't be farther from the truth. Just because someone rejects you does not mean you're rejected. Just because a relationship fails doesn't mean you're not worth deep meaningful relationships. We cannot let the outcome of past relationships determine our future for us.

When a relationship becomes strained, we need to take intentional time in the Presence to get God's heart for the other person. Remember that no matter how you're being treated, how you respond is up to you. First Peter says that even when Jesus was reviled, He did not revile in return. You may really be experiencing mistreatment, but you do not have to take on offense. You do not have to search for revenge or talk badly about the other person. You can simply choose to take it to prayer and move on with your life. Not every person needs to stay in your inner circle forever. Seasons change, people change, and that's okay. Bless them, love them, and let them go.

When you are facing a hard season, you need the right tribe around you. You do not need people around you who are going to blame God. You do not need people around you who want to play "woe is you" and feed into the temptation to choose despair. I am not saying we do not need friends and family who will wrap us in their arms and bring comfort; we absolutely do. Of course, we need those who will mourn with those who mourn. What you need is to know that you can mourn and you can hurt, but while you are in pain, your community is going to help you guard your heart and your mind.

I'll tell my friends, "I love you, but if you can't speak the Truth of the Word in this season, then we might need some space until I'm back on my feet. It is not personal against you, it is guarding my heart and mind toward Him until I can see more clearly."

You have got to come to a place where you are more focused on protecting your relationship with the Father than with your friends. Did you hear that in the back? Community is such an important piece of enduring your trials; make sure it is the *right* community. You have to believe in the promises that God has over your life more than the frustration of your circumstances. You need people who are going to fight for you, not against you. I need friends that know that my priority is Him, so don't just try to make me feel good; call me higher. I realize that what I am saying right now is not easy, but trust me, in times of opposition, you need people around you who will hold up your arms while speaking the Truth. You do not need people who bring a shovel down into the pit and start digging. You need ones who look for a ladder.

If you're struggling to find your tribe, I'm praying for you right now. I'm praying that the right people are going to come into your life. That God is giving you healthy community that you can trust. I'm praying that every wound from past relationships is being healed. Remember, there is a difference between solitude and isolation. There are seasons of our lives when God calls us into solitude to focus on Him and deepen our relationship with Him. These seasons can feel lonely, but they're important for our development. Isolation is when we withdraw to focus on ourselves. This is a place you don't want to be: avoiding community in order to avoid pain. Let go of those past hurts, pray for the right people, and let God fill your life with the right tribe for your season.

9

WILL YOU LEAVE, TOO?

FINALLY, I HAD TO ADMIT IT: I WAS HOPELESS. I HAD LOST ALL HOPE in what I believed. Hope is absolutely vital to us, but I didn't fully realize that until I had none. Amazing what you find out is a necessity after it has been lost. I was on the floor in my parents' home with a bottle of pills in one hand and my Bible in the other. All my fight was gone. I had felt anxiety, fear, depression, pain, and rejection for months. In all of this, He seemed absent and I felt abandoned. He promises to be near the brokenhearted, but I could not understand why He felt so far from me.

As I lay on that floor, I said to Him, "I love You. I just cannot do this anymore. I cannot live another day like this. If You do not show up, I'm done. I quit. I can't deal with this pain anymore."

When I'm telling this story, I like to joke and say that an angel showed up with very large wings to tell me how big my destiny was and assure me that this would pass. I mean, that would be my ideal plot line here. However, that is not what happened at all.

There was no loud boom from heaven. An angel did not show up to encourage me or tell me that my destiny was too big to forfeit. Instead, I had about a ten second moment where I had mental clarity. My head stopped spinning, and I had this one thought pass through my overwhelmed brain: "I don't want to die; I just want the pain to stop."

As fast as the thought came, it left, and all of the confusion and swirl in my brain came rushing back. I fell flat on the floor and wept. One thought. One reality. One moment where the lies stopped and Truth permeated. For the first time in a month, I cried. I had become an emotionless shell. I cried uncontrollably, and sometime later, He spoke.

"Jessika, will you leave me, too?"

I knew that what He said sounded familiar, so I looked it up. It was out of John 6.

Jesus had just preached the most offensive sermon that has ever been preached still to this day. He had been walking with the disciples and showing them the ways of the Kingdom. They had left everything to follow Him and it was starting to pay off. They were growing in relationship with Jesus and seeing miracles. They were finding their purpose as Jesus was teaching them to reveal the Kingdom on earth. People were coming from all around just to hear Jesus speak or ask Him for healing. He was becoming a pretty big deal, and what a privilege for the disciples to be one of His closest friends. I'm sure in their minds, everything was going along perfectly. At this rate, Jesus should be taking His place as King in no time at all and they would be right by His side.

Then Jesus gets up in front of the crowd and tells them that unless they eat His flesh and drink His blood, they would have no part in Him (John 6:56). This is not the sermon topic you would pick to preach if you were trying to become president or grow the largest church in the world. You will not find these words in a church growth program and certainly not in a political campaign ad. This is the type of sermon that gets people removed from platforms. Just as we would expect to happen, the crowd leaves.

I am incredibly grateful for my church and for my pastor. I have received so much from them. I have grown so much. Even with this, if my pastor gets up and tells us that if we want to be part of the church, we would have to drink his blood or eat his flesh, I would leave. I would say,"Thank you for the miracles. Thank you for the transformation. Thank you for all that I received, but it is probably a great time for us to part ways."

It is not shocking that people left Jesus that day. I am probably more shocked that the twelve were left there standing than I am surprised that people left. I would love to believe I'd be standing there with total confidence in Jesus. Truth is, I would have been easily susceptible to follow the crowd.

Jesus, understanding the evident tension, turns to the disciples and says, "Will you leave me, too?"

Peter pipes up with more wisdom than I'm sure he even realized. "Where else would we go? You have the words of life."

This response is remarkable. Peter does not say, "Of course, we aren't leaving Jesu. That was the best sermon you've ever preached!" He does not say, "I totally understand everything you just said, Jesus, and we are on board!" He does not begin to explain communion or give any hint that he has a revelation of what Jesus was referring to. We have nothing to make us think that he gave Jesus a nod and the thumbs up sign expressing comprehension. There was no indication of brave solidarity.

Jesus walked the disciples right into an offensive situation, and instead of assuring them of His great plan, He asks them if they're going to bail. I've studied leadership for years, taught leadership in multiple settings, and I can say as a leader, if I were the one in charge in this moment, I would have taken the disciples aside before the sermon ever started. A nice little pep talk was in order. Something to the effect of, "Hey guys, I'm about to say some stuff that sounds crazy. Don't leave, I'll explain it to you later." If I were to really do what I would want, I would give them the exact play by play and wording. Followed by the reason why I was doing this in the first place. Details provide security and I want my main people to feel totally safe and secure. This passage messes with my leadership style. It means that Jesus' primary goal for His disciples is not their comfort and safety. It means that Jesus did not feel the need to make sure that His closest companions understood Him (ouch!). It also means that He wasn't doing whatever necessary to prevent them from leaving Him (again, ouch!). This passage exemplifies that sometimes Jesus will sometimes be the One who walks us into the circumstances that shake us to our core. We'll talk about this more later, but let me assure you, it is not without purpose. If Jesus walks us into adversity, we must be assured that He always has far greater plans for us than just our simple comfort.

Dear sweet Peter does not in this moment pledge his ultimate allegiance, which we know he is prone to do, but rather he says, "Where else would we go?"

I've heard this preached often as a passionate devotion statement and perhaps that is true. I have started to hear it as an honest question. Where else would we go? In other words, "Jesus, I gave up everything for You! I may not understand why You just did what You did. I may not understand why You're letting this happen. I cannot explain this situation, but I have left behind

WILL YOU LEAVE, TOO? | 55

every other option but You. I have NO PLAN B. You are my only option. Truly, where else would I go?"

I firmly believe that one reason so many people leave Jesus is because they have kept a back up plan in case something doesn't go the way they want it to. When a situation arises that tests their faith or challenges their comfort, there is a temptation to run back to what we have done before. If my pain is too great, I'll run back to that relationship I know you told me to leave. I'll go back to what was comfortable and predictable. I'll run back to that old way of living. If Jesus doesn't work out the way I planned, then I have another option waiting for me. Peter could have gone back to fishing right then, which we know he reverts back to a little later in this story. We have to get to this place like Peter in this moment where we fully abandon every other option but Jesus. Where else would I go? I've laid everything else down. Paul says it this way: "I have been crucified with Christ. It is no longer I who live, but Christ who lives in me. And the life I now live in the flesh I live by faith in the Son of God, who loved me and gave himself for me" (Galatians 2:20 ESV).

If my yes to Jesus comes with conditions, then it never was a yes, it was a maybe. Maybe is a conditional statement. Maybe leaves room to back out. Maybe has options. Maybe says, "Only if my conditions are met will I follow through with my commitment." It is hard for Him to truly be Lord of my life if all He has is my maybe. However, so many people claim Jesus as Lord of their life, yet only truly follow Him when their conditions are met. This is conditional trust. We think conditional trust protects us when in actuality it restrains us. The walls we think are guarding us become the cage we live in.

I cannot urge you enough that when trials come, you must determine within yourself that you will not quit. Adversity is not the time to give up, it is the time to press in. You are allowed to be brokenhearted, in fact, that is when He promises to draw near. You do not have to fake it like everything is okay. You don't have to put on the mask. You can slow down. You can scream. You can cry. Just do not quit.

Joseph was given a dream from the Lord. A dream full of promise and potential. He was so excited about the dream that he shared it with his family. The ones he thought he could trust. The ones that should support him the most. Instead of that dream bringing to pass the greatest season of his life, it brought with it the greatest pressure of his life and a trial that seemed like it would never end. I often wonder what was going through Joseph's brain as he sat in that pit. Surely, he did not initially know how long of an ordeal was ahead of him. Did he think his brothers were playing a prank on him? Of course, they would come back for him in a few minutes? A few hours? As they sold him to the Midianites, did he give up hope then? Maybe he believed that his father would come find him. We aren't given any indication of the emotional battle that Joseph must have been plunged into. He went from a dream, to a pit, to slavery, to prison. There were years sitting in a prison cell, wrongfully accused, betrayed, ignored, equipped with a promise that had seemingly no fruit.

As much as we all wish the fulfillment of our greatest promises came from a journey through green pastures, it is the testing while traveling through the valley of the shadow of death that prepares us for our promotion. God did not prevent the trials in Joseph's life; instead, he used them to prepare Joseph to be a solution for a global problem. As he was able to say on the other side, "You meant this for my harm, but God meant it for good" (Genesis 50:20). Jesus will not prevent all of the trials in your life, but He will use them.

I knew when Jesus asked me that same question He asked the disciples, He was doing to me the same thing He did to them: He was drawing a line in the sand. He was asking me in the moment of my deepest pain I had ever experienced. He was asking me when everything I believed about Him was being tested. In my lowest moment, He wanted to know if I would leave. Just like the disciples, the plan I had was crumbling to pieces and He wanted to know that my commitment was to Him, not to my formulated idea of what life with Him should be like. He was not asking when everything was going exactly the way I wanted it to. He did not ask on my mountaintop. He did not ask when everything made sense. He asked while I was broken and confused. He asked if I was going to keep my decision to choose life. Life and death was set before me again. Would I still choose life now that I was tasting the cost?

I fell into the floor and I wept. I was broken. No matter how broken, I could not leave the One who had built so much history with me. I could not leave the One who had shown me so much love, mercy, and compassion. I was in pain, but that could not and would not erase years of relationship and trust. Like Peter replied, "Where else would we go? You have the words of life."

I don't know why He did not come sit next to me on the floor in the bathroom and hold my hand. I don't know why He didn't wrap me in His arms or even just whisper "I love you" like I had heard Him do hundreds of times before. I don't understand everything He does or doesn't do, but I will say that I am so very grateful now. Often we have an idea of how we think He should show up or respond to our situation, only to realize later He's actually pretty good at leading and loving us. He is kind.

Hope by definition means an expectation or desire for a certain thing to happen. When I had my hope in specific results, I spiraled downward quickly. Just as the Word says, "Hope deferred makes the heart sick (Proverbs 4:23). When we lose hope, we become like a ship in a storm without an anchor. We will be tossed to and fro by thoughts and circumstances. Hebrews calls our hope in Christ an anchor to our souls. Hope brings stability to us in the middle of a storm. The important factor here is hope "in Christ."

When our hope is in Him, we will never be disappointed, but when our hope is in our idea of how our circumstances should be, we risk hope being deferred. Christ is the unshakeable Anchor. The forever constant One. When life is chaotic, He remains the same. The anchor for our souls is hope in the unchanging Person of Jesus Christ. I had put all of my hope in waiting for healing, and up until this point, my hope had been deferred.

Our hope must not be rooted in specific outcomes, but in the nature of the One we follow. This is where our own pride can seep in. We assume we know the best solution for our predicament. If God just answers this prayer, then I would be better. If He would just fix this relationship. If He would give me that job. We place our hope in our best case scenario when our anchor is not a scenario, it's a Savior. When trials come, when your boat starts rocking, guard your heart by anchoring your soul in the hope of Jesus Christ.

When our hopes aren't met and the heart gets sick, we become comfortable with our dysfunction. Normalizing dysfunction makes us think we don't have to face the pain of disappointment. We would rather learn to adjust to our handicap than risk the pain of hope deferred. This decision alone has kept many believers living a life of mediocrity when they were born for greatness. The answer is not to give up on hope and accept a life less than what Jesus paid for. The key is to place my hope in His good nature and trust His ability to work all things for my good, even in my waiting.

Nothing changed in my situation that day, but something changed in me. I gained a new resolve. I was still struggling. Still confused. Still hurting. Still dealing with the same symptoms I had been. Still wishing God would just crash in and fix me. My circumstances remained the same, but my perspective and attitude shifted. Now, quitting was no longer an option.

TIME TO MOVE

WORK HAD BECOME IMPOSSIBLE TO MANAGE. MY PHYSICAL condition made it hard to do anything. My anxiety seemed to follow me into every place that once brought comfort. My world had imploded and I started considering options to move.

At first, all I wanted to do was buckle down and wait until things got better. I wanted to prove I could fix this. Now it was evident it would not work out that way. Can I tell you that sometimes God will use these adverse circumstances to move you to the right location for His breakthrough? He knows that unless we become uncomfortable, we will stay right where we are. He lets circumstances plunge us into being so uncomfortable that we'll finally allow Him to move us.

I spoke to a few friends and started exploring some different options. I considered going back on the mission field. That was one place I knew I always heard Him. Thankfully, everyone around me discouraged that idea.

I had tried healing evangelists, I had tried prayer, I had even tried a little bit of counseling. I wondered if I needed to just accept my lot and learn to live with my condition.

A few friends suggested I try a visit to Bethel Church because they had been known for seeing miracles. They were also good friends of IRIS Ministries who I had worked with. I was hesitant to go for more prayer lines, oil blessings, and shakarabas, but at this point, everything felt like it could be an option.

One day, I was supposed to volunteer at a lunch for veterans. I was not looking forward to it at all. I had promised my mom we would do it together, and I did not want to let her down. She and my family were already putting up with so much from me. I sat in the front seat of her car as she drove us, gazing out the window, already fighting back the urge to break into hysterics. We walked into the building and she went to go chat to a few people she knew. My vision began to narrow and everything started going black. I put my back against the wall and began to shrink down to the floor. I could not breathe. I could not see. I did not think I was going to make it. It felt like I was having a heart attack. My mom came around the corner and found me as I burst into tears telling her I could not do it. I could not stay. I had to leave. As embarrassing and horrible as this situation was, it was finally what I needed to seek help. It was my proverbial rock bottom.

She took me home to stay with my father while she went back to volunteer at the banquet. For the first time since this ordeal started, I allowed my dad to see how bad I was doing. I cried and told him I did not know what to do. He asked me one question: What did I need to get better? Before I even had the chance to think of an answer, I told him I needed to get to Bethel Church. I have no idea why that came out of my mouth. I'm now convinced that Holy Spirit was not going to let me miss what God was preparing for me. My dad told me he would pay for it and do whatever I needed to get help. I applied to Bethel School of Supernatural Ministry and was accepted just a few days later.

In just a month's time, I packed up my car and headed for California. I was moving out of desperation. Friends had told me that this church in Redding would be able to help me. At the time, I did not know much about the church or the school, but at the slight chance they could help, I decided to give it a shot. My plan was to hurry up, get healed, and get back to the life I was comfortable with. As I've said, I had no idea what was really going on inside of me. I just thought I had extreme post traumatic stress and I needed to quickly be healed so that I could go back to my "normal" way of life. I needed to go back to war zones, back to preaching, back to being the one who had it all together. I needed me back. I wasn't looking forward to what God had ahead of me, I was clinging to my past and screaming for what I called normal.

When I moved, I had to lay down so many things that mattered to me. I left a job that I loved. I cancelled so many plans for trips and projects. I left while the relationship with my best friend was still severely strained. I left my friends and family behind. I had hoped that I would move, get some sort of help, and then hurry back to Texas to try and put the pieces of my life back together. I've since learned that we're often begging God to repair something when He wants to exchange it.

I mentioned earlier, Jesus is the Great Exchanger. He took death from you and gave life. He takes our burdens and gives rest. You see, Jesus actually enjoys taking things from you. He never takes with intention to steal from you, but rather to bless you. The devil wants to take from you in order to rob from your life; Jesus takes things from you in order to bring upgrades. It is only in abiding that we can discern the difference.

I find in myself the desire to latch onto what is being taken away from me even when it is Jesus taking it. My humanity still fights against the notion that when Jesus takes something, He has good intentions in mind. I somehow have the belief that I know better than He does what should and should not be in my life. One of my heroes, Corrie Ten Boom, said, "I hold onto things loosely, so that it doesn't hurt so bad when Jesus pries them from my fingers." I remember reading the quote when I was younger thinking that Jesus would never pry anything from your fingers. How rude! Now after serving Him for fifteen years, I've found He will indeed take things that are no longer necessary in my life, but He does prefer me to surrender them.

Isn't this one of the most beautiful aspects of Jesus, even though it can be painful? He asks for our lives, not just portions of it. He promises to take the things we do not want and replace them for things we very much do. For instance, He takes our ashes and gives us beauty. He gives joy for mourning. He takes our heaviness and gives a garment of praise (Isaiah 61:3). We love these promises and trust in His faithfulness to fulfill them. Then when He asks for something from us that we're more fond of, something that doesn't feel like ashes to us, that's when this whole thing gets complicated. He will ask us to surrender things that we would rather keep. He will ask you for relationships. He will ask you for that job. He'll ask you for that place of comfort. Even in the harder exchanges, we must not forget His nature. When God asks you to surrender, or takes something from you, it is always to bring you something better and draw you closer to Him. He is a good Father that knows perfectly how to parent His children. Trust Him.

At Bethel, people began to encourage me to be vulnerable with them about what was going on with me, which by the way, I hated. Hate doesn't even seem like strong enough of a word. It went against everything I had been taught by previous leaders. In many churches, we discourage vulnerability for fear that we will negate faith. I was instructed to ask myself why I was feeling what I was feeling. I thought that was stupid. Why in the world do I need to ask myself what I was feeling? Can't I just feel it? Aren't feelings just feelings, unimportant to the Kingdom? I did not see emotions as having any eternal value, and therefore, completely unnecessary for my holy work of serving Jesus.

He started a process where I had to learn that God is actually emotional. He feels. We cannot possibly get through the Gospels without seeing that Jesus had emotions, but somehow I had missed it. It is amazing how much we will miss in the nature of Jesus when we read Scripture to affirm our theology rather than to encounter Him. He made us to feel. Emotions are not our Truth, however, they are often used by God for a purpose. Choosing to totally ignore those emotions is dangerous.

Pain isn't fun. Pain isn't easy. However, pain is simply going to come in life. How we choose to view pain and deal with pain will play a major role in our overall ability to run this race for the long haul. I thought my story would be that I came to Bethel, got healed, the pain would leave, and I would, too—straight back to Texas. Instead, I was about to dive even deeper into vulnerability, pain, and emotions, just like Jesus had planned.

NOT WHAT I HOPED FOR

WHILE EVERYONE ELSE IN THEIR FIRST YEAR OF MINISTRY SCHOOL seemed to be having the time of their lives, I spent the first month falling deeper into depression. I would look around at everyone jumping with excitement while I was on the side of the room bawling my eyes out. Taking a girl with massive anxiety from trauma and putting her in a room of over one thousand really excited students does not seem like a great plan, but many of God's plans are like this. What can seem like horrible ideas in the natural are often the perfect recipe for God to do the supernatural.

Not only was going to school hard on my emotions, it was also hard on my body. After arriving in Redding, I found out that on top of the effects from post traumatic stress disorder, I also had adrenal fatigue. Everyday, it would take all of my energy to get up out of bed to go to school. I would come home to position myself on the couch and stay there until I fell asleep, sometimes as early as five in the afternoon. My roommates liked to call me 'grandma,' which was a decently accurate description.

One afternoon during my first year at BSSM, I left early from school and came home to fall asleep on the couch. It was one of my hard days. As I lay on that couch, I remember just thinking that I would never be able to do anything for God ever again. I felt useless. If I couldn't even make it through a day at school, then what was the point in me being there? I began to cry as I wallowed in my self pity. In my heart, I was hurting because I felt like I had nothing of value to offer the Lord. As I lay there with tears streaming down my face, God spoke to me. He said, "Jessika, you are as valuable to Me laying on the couch as you are behind a pulpit or in the nations."

I had spent years traveling to nations, preaching the Gospel, loving the poor. Without even noticing, I had begun to define myself by my assignments. I actually loved what I did and loved that people saw me as the "nations girl," the "war zone missionary," or the preacher. It had become my identity. It is easy to fall into the trap of finding our identity in what we do for God instead of who we are to Him. The problem with defining yourself by your calling is that when you can no longer perform, you don't know who you are. So here I was on a couch, unable to do anything for Him, and He was redefining my value. If my value was only in what fruit I could produce for Him, then I was worth nothing. If it was found in the price He paid for me, then I was worth everything.

Jesus died for me and you so that He could have all of us. He died knowing every high and every low moment of my life. He chose to die knowing that I would fail. He chose knowing I would be weak. He knew exactly what He was getting into and He still chose the cross, He still chose me. It is liberating when we realize that Jesus didn't just die for the best version of you, He also died for the worst version. When I decide that He is Lord of my life, then I give up the right to believe that I am worth anything less than what He was willing to pay for me. God gave Jesus and that is too high of a price to think I am only valuable when I can be used in "ministry." Especially my small limited view of ministry at the time. At twenty six years old, being unable to get off the couch felt like a death sentence. It was hard to put into perspective that this was a temporary moment that did not disqualify my future. What was meant to only be a season felt like a lifetime diagnosis. The greatest news is that our value is not determined in our weakest moment. It is also not determined by our strongest moment. It is only determined by the cross.

A girl I had only met a couple of times approached me while I was on the couch one afternoon and said she had a dream where I was going to a place called the "Destiny House." I had heard about the house before and knew that they were a community house that would worship together every Friday. The girl offered to come pick me up and take me that week. As much as I was dreading it, I went. It was a high price to pay—Friday was my day off of school. It was the day I needed to sleep in, let my body recoup, and most importantly, avoid people at all costs.

Destiny House was located in a three story house where they used the middle floor each week to invite people to come in and join them for two hours of intimate worship. Everyone would crowd in and focus on His Presence. It actually was beautiful.

I soon found out Destiny House was closely connected with IRIS ministries and most of the people in the house had a heart for missions. At the time, I wanted absolutely nothing to do with anyone doing missions, nor did I want anyone to know the things I had done in the nations. I would come in to have a few short conversations with people and find a place for myself in a corner where I could be left alone.

During worship that first day, my anxiety lifted, and for the first time in months, I felt peace. I began to look forward to these few moments all week long. I knew if I could just make it through to Friday, then I would have a couple hours of reprieve from my wicked anxiety. I was no longer looking for healing. I had found this sliver of hope for a two-hour period once a week, and that little bit of hope gave me what I needed to manage what I thought was my new life. These moments took me from dying to surviving. I felt better than I had in months, but I had no idea that God was orchestrating so much more.

DANCE OVER ME

DURING TRIALS, WE HAVE AN OPPORTUNITY WE'LL NEVER HAVE AGAIN in heaven: the opportunity to offer a fragrance of worship while we are in pain. In heaven, there will be no more adversity, no more death and destruction, so only for as long as we are on this earth can we offer this type of worship—a worship that says to God that He is still worthy even when life may be painful. It is not always easy to feel the weight of disappointment or confusion and still choose to worship. It takes us realizing that though our circumstances may change, He does not. He is always worthy, always deserving, always faithful. The temptation in trials is to solely focus on our emotions instead of who He is. When we fix our eyes on Jesus, the natural response is to worship—not because we enjoy our circumstances, but because of our awareness of Him.

One week during worship at Destiny House, a girl walked over to me and asked me if she could dance over me. I had no idea what that even meant, and I hated the idea. She wanted to put me in the middle of the room with all the attention on me while she did some kind of weird dance? Worst idea ever. But... I'm from Texas. Texans have ingrained in them that we should be nice to people whenever possible. I didn't want to hurt this girl's feelings, so despite all my better judgment, I said yes. I went to the middle of the room, crossed my legs, and began to beg God to make this crazy woman hurry up. I did not know what she thought this was going to do, and all I wanted was her to stop interrupting my two hours of peace. This was my two hours. My precious two hours. To waste even a few minutes of it felt like a high cost.

She began to dance over me, and very shortly, I began to feel physical weights falling off my shoulders. I began to feel lighter. I did not even know how heavy I felt until the burdens were being lifted off of me. I felt a claw pull out of my back and I started weeping uncontrollably, falling like a puddle onto the floor. A group of people came over and began to pray for me. I don't remember a single thing that was said. God was powerfully encountering me while I was in that mess right there in front of everyone.

After a while, the flow of the morning changed. I went back to my corner and we finished worship. I drove home that day and told my roommates that I knew something had changed. I did not know what, I just knew something was different. I went to bed that night and had no nightmares. I woke up the next day and had no anxiety. Over the next few days, I realized that every single side effect of PTSD was gone.

I was healed.

It only takes one moment for God to totally transform your situation and your life. We never know how close we are to that moment of breakthrough. We never know how God will do it or who He will use.

I spent the next few days wondering each day if that would be the day that my anxiety would come back. After months of living in pain, I had to relearn how to live without it. Even though I had just had a life-changing healing encounter, I did not know how to believe that I was actually better. I had to face the fact that I had become hopeless. I had forgotten how to have hope for the days ahead. I did not remember who I was apart from my disorder. I was healed, but I had no idea what to do next.

I was healed of all physical effects of post traumatic stress disorder that very day when I was danced over (note, it still feels awkward to say I was "danced over"), however, there was so much more for me to learn from this dark season—as if learning that God healed people through dance wasn't enough. Over the course of months and eventually years, God began to show me the purpose in my pain. He showed me what part I had played in some of the turmoil that had ripped through my life. Ultimately, He rebuilt the ground beneath me that had cracked and nearly given way under the pressures of my trials. As painful and devastating as this time period was, it also revealed those cracks. It put a spotlight on my areas of dysfunction and weakness. It reminded me that I am absolutely forever dependent on God for life and, remarkably, I have a tendency to forget that.

GOD'S PRESENCE OR PROMISE?

"Then the Lord said to Moses, 'Leave this place, you and the people you brought up out of Egypt, and go up to the land I promised on oath to Abraham, Isaac and Jacob, saying, "I will give it to your descendants." I will send an angel before you and drive out the Canaanites, Amorites, Hittites, Perizzites, Hivites and Jebusites. Go up to the land flowing with milk and honey. But I will not go with you.'" (Exodus 33:1-3)

"If Your Presence does not go with us, do not bring us up from here." (Exodus 33:15)

If everything you longed for and everything you were promised was offered to you to claim as your own without a battle, how hard would it be to turn it down? The wilderness had been a place of hardship specifically for Moses. It was a place of frustration. God offered Moses a quick and easy way out of his trial. You probably did not catch what I just said. Let me emphasize, GOD OFFERED Moses a QUICK and EASY way out of his trial. I did not say the *enemy* offered him a way out. *God* did. Not only would he get to be done with this painfully long trial, he would walk easily into the season of his dreams, the season of Promise.

What is it that you have been promised? A thriving business? Influence in certain spheres? A family? A ministry with plenty of resources? What if today God offered for you to have that all tomorrow without any more pain or fight? He actually assures you that an angel will go before you and every obstacle that would attempt to stand in your way will be removed for you. You simply have to walk right into your Promise Land. The only catch is that He will not go with you.

We like to assume that this would be an easy choice. Oh, of course, I would turn it down, I want Jesus or nothing else! We Christians have great mantras for battle when we're not in the battle. I wish I could say with certainty that my initial response would be like Moses': Give me Your Presence or nothing at all. I love Him, you love Him—wouldn't the natural response be to stay where He is? But all too often, we confuse the Promised Land with the Promiser. If there were an easy button to our dreams, most of us would press that button without a thought, because the assumption would be that receiving the Promise means we have the Presence. Is that true, though?

Oswald Chambers says, "I find that temptation in my own life is often just a shortcut to my highest goal." Moses knew that God would be faithful to His promise. He knew that one day the Israelites would indeed make it into the Promised Land and that God would be with them. He was being offered a way to get there immediately. A way to get out of the painful season now. The offer was a shortcut. It tested the affection of Moses' heart. What did he really want in life? Did he want the Promise or the Presence? TD Jakes says, "We're a microwave generation serving a crockpot God." Ouch. I want my portion and I want it now. I don't want to marinate in the heat for hours and hours. Hit the popcorn button and let's get pumping out those promises. In this generation, we are heavily influenced by social media. We are used to being able to hit a button and get instant results. I see so many people that are more concerned with their life looking successful than it actually being successful. We're searching for perfectly lighted pictures to post so that we can get instant affirmation from our social media following and we're far less concerned with building a life that will actually reap heavenly rewards.

> "He thought it was better to suffer for the sake of Christ than to own the treasures of Egypt, for he was looking ahead to his great reward." (Hebrews 11:26 NLT)

I want the Presence of God. There are also so many promises from Him that I want, as well. I press in for them. I believe for them. I pray over them. I am willing to fight giants for them. But if my desire to escape discomfort surpasses my desire for His Presence, then I will undoubtedly take any shortcut offered to me and call it a blessing. When that happens, it often takes a while for people to even realize that the Presence left while they were focused on taking their promise. I would hate to get to heaven and God say, "Well, you sure made people think you were living in my will. Your Instagram looks like you prioritized my Presence." Yikes!

In adversity, I had definitely become more focused on my promise than His presence. My hope was not in Him, it was totally focused on my circumstances changing. It is hard to admit, but when I look back, I know that if I were given the option to be totally healed and restored or have His Presence, I probably would have taken the healing.

I honestly thought I was someone totally different than the person who came out in the fire. The pain and discomfort had stolen my attention from the Presence. My devotion had become diluted to the point where I wanted His hand more than I wanted His heart. It took this painful trial for me to see what was actually in my heart, and then I had to deal with it. Ugh. Can't He just fix us in an instant? But the work of sanctification is just that: work. Anyone who tells you it's not is flat out a liar. He who began a good work in you will see it through to completion, and at the same time, we must work out our salvation with fear and trembling. I hate to break it to you (if I'm the first one to ever tell you), but you actually have to take part in your growth.

I want to encourage you that if you are still in the midst of your trial, one of the first things we must do is focus on Him. We must not be so focused on our desire to be out of our circumstances that we make the promise of our healing or deliverance of greater priority. We must not be in a rush to get back to our insta-perfect life. The only thing that is guaranteed to go with you into your next season is the history you've built with Him. So no matter how difficult the trials of your life are right now, don't forget to focus your attention on Him. Make it a top priority to continue building a history with Him that will undoubtedly outlast your current circumstances.

Then, as your eyes are refocused on Him, you can see your circumstances more clearly. You can see where God is moving. You can hear what He is doing. You can begin to partner with His plans for your season. Make no mistake about it: no matter how difficult the trials of life are, God is working.

GOD ON TRIAL

THE COURTROOM WAS SET AND IT WAS TIME FOR THE TRIAL TO TAKE place. I was walking in ready to take my place at the defendant's bench. The guilt seemed too heavy to bear. Have you ever had that feeling in the pit of your stomach where you just knew that you were guilty? I walked in with my head down, avoiding looking anyone in the eyes, guided by a man presumably in charge of me. My shame was tangible. As I glanced quickly to the left and the right, it seemed that the court-room is packed. Who would have thought that my trial would be so important? All I knew was, I was dreading this.

As I walked up the center aisle, ready to turn and take my seat, I was more than aware that this wouldn't be much of a trial. Even I knew that I deserved it. I deserved to be found guilty. I wondered what the punishment was going to be. As I approached the table to take my seat, my attention was grabbed by a bright red blood line smeared on the ground in between me and my seat. I looked up, confused and uncertain. As I looked up to what I assumed to be my chair, I realized something astonishing: someone was already sitting in the seat of the accused. It was God. God was sitting in the seat of the defendant. The man with me gently pulled my arm in the direction of the front of the courtroom and I followed.

Places have been taken for the defendant and the prosecution. There's a line of witnesses eagerly awaiting to testify, and the next thing I know, I'm ushered to the seat of the judge. When I looked up from the judge's bench, it was still God who was sitting in the defendant's chair.

How was it possible that I was sitting as judge and GOD was sitting in the seat of the accused?

God spoke to me and said, "Jessika, the enemy no longer has the ability to accuse you to Me. The blood of Jesus has been shed on your behalf and when I look at you, I see that blood. He cannot accuse you to Me, so instead he will accuse Me to you."

And then the vision ended.

When the vision was over, many memories began to flash through my mind. What were the thoughts I had throughout this chaotic season? Oh yes, I remember now: absolute cynicism and negativity. The once optimistic and hopeful Jessika turned into someone that would be more fitting with a group of doomsday believers. I didn't meditate on anything that resembled that Philippians 4 verse that we cherish: *Whatever is pure, whatever is noble, think on these things.* I found myself in the area of *whatever is the opposite of everything you said you believed*, not just in conversation, but from a stinking pulpit, for crying out loud. I became so utterly hopeless in my thoughts that I spent most of my time waiting for another blow. I couldn't muster enough to believe He might want to use these circumstances for others. When I wasn't being healed, I began to question Him and everything I had believed about Him.

Instead of meditating on anything remotely positive, I was asking myself questions like, "If God is good, why are children dying in wars they had no choice in being part of?" and "If God is my peace, then why do I feel so anxious?" On any given day, my thought life was assaulting the nature of God thousands of times, each witness testifying against Him with examples from my history, my emotions, and my fear of the future. A case was being built in my mind and my heart, and I didn't even know that I was acknowledging the witnesses of the prosecution, the witnesses of the enemy.

I know, you reading this have probably never struggled with this sort of snowball of negativity. I'm just trying to help you see how far gone I was. If there was hope for me, then surely there's hope for you.

Have you ever noticed that when things aren't going quite right, there is a barrage of negative thoughts that seem to come from nowhere? Make no mistake about it, the enemy is on the prowl and he is calling his witnesses to the stand. The thoughts come so quickly, they feel so real, and yet they're in such contradiction with everything you had believed to be true.

Not once had I ever thought that in the midst of my trial, perhaps I was not the one being accused. Is it possible that perhaps life is a little bit less about me than I thought it was? When trials come (or let's be real, just in life in general), there is a temptation to believe that the earth is revolving around us. I am the most important thing in this equation. We unintentionally create a victim mentality where everything in life is out to get us. Unfortunately, there actually are no "one man" shows in life. Newsflash, Jessika: I am not the most important thing on the planet. Bummer.

When the blood of Jesus was shed, Satan no longer had the

ability to accuse any man who accepted the gift of salvation. He knows that any attempt to do so in the court would be futile because we're covered in the blood of Jesus. The verdict has already been given: we, my friends, have been found not guilty.

> "So now the case is closed. There remains no accusing voice of condemnation against those who are joined in life-union with Jesus, the Anointed One." (Romans 8:1 TPT)

It is easy to glaze over this reality as a simple truth we've heard a million times. I wouldn't ever want us to get to a point where the Gospel no longer impacts our hearts. The blood of Jesus, the most powerful drops of liquid in all of history, shed on our behalf. It defies all logic and achieves the inconceivable. Listen, I know all too well how guilty I am. How deserving of punishment I am. I can't afford to take His sacrifice lightly and neither can you. I live everyday in the effects of His choice to lay down His life. Why would I want to willingly put myself back in a place of condemnation? Doing so is an actual affront to the cross. It is saying to Jesus that His sacrifice was not enough. "Your beating didn't accomplish enough; I think I'll beat myself up a little bit, too!" How ludicrous is this? His blood was, is, and always will be more than enough to cover my sins. This is the beauty of the cross. The Guiltless One paid for my sin. How dare I try to pay for what has already been paid for as if it weren't enough.

Often times, we're unaware that we're even a participant in the court case. A trial is going on, we are the judge, and we are totally unaware that we have any authority whatsoever. When my nightmares were severe, my thought life seemed to be taking a negative turn without me even noticing. My emotions were controlling everything.

There's a reason the Bible exhorts us to meditate on His Word, to think on what is pure, to take every thought captive—and it isn't because God is some egotistical leader that demands constant attention. It is because without a guard on duty, the enemy will begin to infiltrate the battleground of our minds, often unbeknownst to us. He will plant lies that he intends to ultimately use to sabotage our future.

The enemy cannot accuse you to God, so instead he will attempt to accuse God to you. And this is why God is sitting in the seat of the defendant. The enemy is constantly plotting a violent assault on your beliefs on the nature of God. There's good news, my friend: you are the judge and you have the authority to call your own witnesses to the stand. We don't have to sit and listen to witnesses who have been assigned to lie, accuse, and distort the truth. You don't have to idly consent to thoughts that contradict His true nature. In fact, I encourage you to slam your gavel down sooner rather than later and allow no slander in the courtroom of your mind. It's your turn to call some witnesses to the stand.

David found himself in this courtroom countless times throughout Scripture. One of my favorite passages is in Psalm 103. Once again, David found himself in a hard spot. After making his fair share of mistakes, he was battling the voices of the accuser. Satan was attacking the nature of God, but also David himself. Psalm 103 plays out like testimony in a courtroom.

You see, the enemy does not have the ability to accuse you to God, but this does not mean that in the trials of our lives, he won't accuse us, to us. Imagine with me the lies attacking David's mind. The shame and guilt from his own shortcomings. The temptation to doubt if God will show up for him again. What does David do? Let's look at the passage:

"Bless the LORD, O my soul, and all that is within me, bless his holy name!" (Psalm 103:1 ESV)

David, in his heartache, in his trial, in his weakness, begins to speak to his soul. In the world, they say you're crazy if you talk to yourself; in the Kingdom, you're stupid if you don't. David decided in the courtroom of his trial that it was time to call his own witnesses to the stand. I highly doubt his emotions felt like it; he just knew he had to take authority in his mind. As he speaks to himself to bless the Lord, what does he begin to declare?

"Bless the Lord, O my soul, and forget not all his benefits!"

He stands up and says to himself, :Bless Him and do not forget all that He has done for you. Do not forget who He really is." Then David begins to call each witness to the stand.

"...who forgives all your iniquity, who heals all your diseases, who redeems your life from the pit, who crowns you with steadfast love and mercy, who satisfies you with good so that your youth is renewed like the eagle."

David continues on verse by verse declaring the nature of God in spite of his current circumstances. He still felt the sting of his sin and yet he declared God's forgiveness. He felt the sickness of disease and the depression of being in the pit. Though he was not yet delivered, he reminded his soul of the nature of God. This is the nature of faith. Bill Johnson says, "Faith does not deny a problem's existence; it denies it influence."

When the trials of life, like David's, lead us into the courtroom of our mind, we do not need to deny the reality of our circumstances; we just deny them influence. We do this by focusing on the nature of God. Revelation 12:11 says that "they overcome by the blood of the Lamb and the Word of their testimony." We have the blood of Jesus, and now is when you need to call your witnesses to the stand, the Word of your testimony.

In the next chapter, we'll talk about the invitation we find in these assaults on His nature, but for now, let's focus on the types of testimony we have to call to the stand, the number one source of testimony always being the Word. Throughout the Bible, we find verses and stories that testify to who He is. These are our ammunition against the enemy's attacks on His nature. When I am battling thoughts of accusation, I find Scripture that deals with that specific lie and I declare it out loud over and over until I believe it. Sometimes I start off by saying it literally thousands of times a day, but I am unwilling to fall into the trap of believing the enemy's lies again.

The second source of testimony is our history with God. I look back on my life and I recount all the times that God has shown up for me. I write those testimonies out and I remind myself of them when I start feeling doubtful or worried. If I'm struggling financially, I remind myself of all the times He has provided. If I'm sick, I remind myself of all the times He has healed me. I write out each of these testimonies and read them multiple times a day. If I need to, I record them and play them on repeat.

The final source of testimony is to listen to the testimonies of how God has showed up for others. God is no respecter of persons (Acts 10:34). What He has done for one, He will do for another. The testimony of Jesus is the spirit of prophecy (Revelation 19:10). So I reach out to others who have been through similar situations and have overcome. I ask them to share with me what God has done in their situations and ask them to pray for a release of that testimony into my life. This requires humility and vulnerability on my part. I have to be willing to share my struggle and honor the breakthrough that someone else is carrying.

As we use these sources of testimony against the witnesses of the enemy, we become saturated in truth instead of lies, and it is the truth that will set us free.

DIVINE SET-UPS

"In the same way that gold and silver are refined by fire, the Lord purifies your heart by the tests and trials of life." (Proverbs 17:3 TPT)

WE MUST FIGHT TO NOT ALLOW OURSELVES TO SLIP INTO A SPIRIT OF grief that sees no hope. I allowed the pain and confusion I was experiencing to have influence. After having done all to stand, I laid down in the valley of the shadow of death. I pitched a tent. I found a sleeping bag. I decided I might as well just make a home there. But that valley was never meant to be a camping ground. We are to walk through this valley until we're out on the other side.

I'm not being vulnerable about my weaknesses and failures just for your entertainment. I'm being honest because maybe you've been there, too. Maybe, just maybe, you've done the Ephesians 6 thing when having done all to stand, you continued to stand, and for some reason, it still didn't seem to be working. It felt like nothing was changing. Like me, maybe you wrote out all the declarations, all the promises, you went through the healing line hundreds of times and put your name on all the prayer lists. You're reading this right now and you can identify with the pain of disappointment. You have felt the hopelessness of circumstances not changing. You recognize the confusion of when it doesn't seem to work. I refuse to pretend like my story didn't involve a very long period of "I don't know what the h*** is going on." It did. What I didn't know was that my trials were actually an invitation.

James instructs us to have joy in trials (James 1:2). Personally, I used to find this verse to be one of the most perplexing verses in the entire Bible. I think it's clear to see that I hardly found my trials something that sparked even a hint of joy. If your trials have been anything like mine, then perhaps you also found yourself in the fetal position more times then you'd like to admit. So how is it that James actually thinks we can find joy in trials? Let's look into the following verses:

> "Count it all joy, my brothers, when you meet trials of various kinds, FOR YOU KNOW that the testing of your faith produces steadfastness. And let steadfastness have its full effect that you may be perfect and complete, lacking nothing." (James 1:2-4, emphasis added)

James sees our trials as an invitation. It is through trials that we receive from the Lord. Trials are producing a road for us that leads to us being "perfect and complete, lacking nothing." In other words, trials are a divine set-up for increase and growth.

We already know that our trials attempt to attack the nature of God, but what if our trials were actually an invitation to experience the nature of God that is being attacked? What if the very thing the enemy wants to stop in us is what propels us forward?

Think about it like this: without being sick, I couldn't have such a tangible encounter with Him as healer. Without feeling rejected, I couldn't have really known Him so deeply as a Father who accepts me. Without making mistakes, we can't really have such a great appreciation for His nature to forgive. Jesus speaks to this in the parable of the two debtors when He asks Simon who loves more, the one who is forgiven of just a little or the one who is forgiven of much? Those who experience adversity understand God's nature more deeply than those who have only known ease. Our need for certain aspects of His nature are revealed when they are tested.

The moment of trial you're in right now, no matter how painful, is actually a great indication of how God wants to reveal Himself to you. Your trial is an invitation to see a new aspect of God's nature that perhaps you've never experienced before. Graham Cooke says, "With every new season I ask God who He wants to be to me in my current season that He couldn't be in the last one." friend?

I consider this the theory of opposite natures. When I am experiencing a trial that seems to contradict a specific aspect of God's Word and nature, I know that God wants to come in and show Himself as the opposite of what the enemy is trying to convince me He is. In anxiety, God wants to be peace. In depression, God wants to be our joy. In lack, God wants to be Provider. What is the area in your life that God's nature is being challenged? I believe that is the very area in which God wants to show up and prove Himself to you. Instead of dwelling on my area of need, let's focus on who God wants to be. Let's look at this trial as an invitation.

The first way to put this into motion is by practicing gratefulness. Gratefulness is one of our most powerful tools in every season of life, but especially during trials. James says to have joy in trial BECAUSE we know that there is something promised on the other side. I may not be able to be grateful for the adversity, but I can be grateful for the promise on the other side of it.

When I am facing a difficulty, the first thing I do is turn on gratefulness. I start telling God how thankful I am for the gifts in my life. I recount the many things that are going right even though some things may be going wrong. I start looking for what God is wanting to do through the trial and I praise Him in advance for it.

How frustrating for the enemy that his attempts to defeat us move us to a place of extreme gratefulness! What a slap in his face that his ugly schemes push us closer to the nature of the Father when he was trying to pull us away. There is nothing I enjoy more than watching the plans of the enemy be used for God's purposes. I believe we will all be able to say like Joseph, "You meant this for evil against me, but God meant it for good…" (Genesis 50:20).

MAKE THE ENEMY PAY

"Jessika, if the enemy had known what I was going to do through this, he would not have attacked you in the first place." It was so similar to the verse in Corinthians that says, "Had the powers of darkness known they would not have crucified the Lamb of glory."

Excuse me? Had He seen me recently? He spoke this not long after my healing. Yeah, the nightmares had stopped and I wasn't looking for the next opportunity to kill myself, but I would hardly say that the enemy regretted his attack. In fact, thanks to me, he was probably quite proud of himself. He probably put my poster up in hell as training for demons on how to partner with humans to utterly screw up their lives. I was still battling adrenal fatigue and constantly learning where my physical limits were with my recovering body. I was grateful, oh so grateful for my healing, but I was still learning to live like a normal human being again. You know, like how normal people get up in the morning, shower, get dressed, eat, and go do something other than spend their entire day trying to breathe. I wasn't even thinking about what the next phase of life would look like and I certainly wasn't looking to pick a fight with hell. I was tired of fighting.

Can you imagine how much the enemy regrets crucifying Jesus? It is probably number two on his regret list right next to choosing to defy God in heaven. Now God was telling me that the enemy would regret attacking me? It took awhile for me to get on board with what He was promising. Day after day, He kept telling me that He was going to make the enemy pay. It soon became a promise I latched onto when it did not seem possible at all. I was still sleeping at least twelve hours a day as my body tried to recoup from months of sleep deprivation. I was still battling thoughts of inadequacy and struggling to believe in a hopeful future. He had just healed me in the most bizarre way, though, and I couldn't help but think that maybe it was time to start trusting Him again.

This is why it is imperative in moments of trial that we take time to be with Him. Even when our mind is screaming, we must quiet ourselves and abide. In John 15, we have a promise that if we abide, then our prayers will be answered. He also promises that if we abide, we will find joy. When we are in pain, we often look for quick and easy distractions to take our mind off of our circumstances. Netflix binging and Instagram scrolling becomes the numbing escape plan. Though that is not inherently wrong to do, we cannot neglect the secret place.

You need a Word from heaven for your season. You need to know what Jesus is saying for you, right now, right where you are. Jesus went around destroying the works of the enemy, the Bible says. Everywhere He went, He was wreaking havoc on the kingdom of darkness. In regions where the enemy had years of strongholds, Jesus came in and entire cities were being converted and set free. Diseases were being healed, demons were being cast out, brokenness was being restored. He was literally the enemy's worst nightmare. He was revealing the true nature of the Father on earth.

It is not shocking that Satan decided he needed an extreme plan to deal with this extreme adversary named Jesus. This set about the crucifixion plan. If Jesus is going around destroying all of their plans, then the enemy thought, let's just find a way to destroy Him. He probably assumed that if he took out Jesus, then the rest of the disciples would eventually scatter back into their former lifestyles. He just needed to kill Jesus. Cut off the Head and a body will not function.

We know that Jesus said that no one took His life, rather He willingly laid it down (John 10:18). It is laughable to me that the enemy thought for a second that he would be able to kill God on earth. I wonder why it was never shocking that the enemy thought he could stop the plans of God for my life or for yours? Nonetheless, we find ourselves in the place where Jesus is going to be crucified.

I am clearly a dramatic person, so when I envision this moment, I often wonder what is going on in hell. The verse says that if they would have known what was going to happen, they wouldn't have crucified Him, so in my mind, they are completely unaware up until the moment that Jesus takes that last breath. Then chaos ensues. I call this interpretation the JTV or "Jessika Tate Version." There is no biblical basis for this, but humor me. I picture that as Jesus is taking His last breath, the demons in hell were ready for a big party celebrating the victory they thought they had won. The tormentors in hell have a big screen television watching with expectation. Surely, there's some sort of webcam to earth. The ones roaming earth want to be at the cross to celebrate with the others. Every single demonic principality is eagerly anticipating the moment that He breathes His last breath on earth. Jesus breathes in and there was about 0.2 seconds of rejoicing before they realized they had made one horrible mistake. Jesus takes that last breath and everything changes. He shows up to release the captives in prison, bodies come out of their graves, the earth itself shifts as life as it had been known was undergoing a dramatic change.

We know the rest of the story. Jesus defeated sin and death for us and we can now declare, "Oh death where is your sting?" (1 Corinthians 15:55).

When Jesus was alive, He told the disciples that it was better for them that He leave. At the time, this would be such a confusing statement. The disciples had left everything to follow Jesus. They had pledged their allegiance to Him. They had their own ideas of how He would rule and reign. Now He is telling them that He is going to leave, and not only is He going to leave, but it will be better for them if He does. That would be a frustrating statement. How could life be better if He is gone? What would we live for if He was gone?

Often in life, we will find ourselves in comparable moments — times when how we thought life was going to turn out turns into circumstances that seem directly opposite to our dreams. These moments are defining. What do we believe when it feels like everything we had dreamed for crashes down? What do we say when it feels like the promise has slipped through our fingers? What does it look like in the moment between Friday and Sunday?

Obviously, Jesus resurrects, He comes back to fulfill His promises. He encourages the disciples to wait because there was more to come. Then we have Pentecost, the Holy Spirit is poured out on flesh. The very Godhead is now dwelling inside of man. What a phenomenon.

Here is where we really begin to understand just how much the enemy regrets crucifying Jesus. At first, the enemy had one major problem named Jesus. Now, all of these "believers" were being filled with the exact same power that Jesus had. In Satan's attempt to stop the Kingdom from advancing, he actually propelled it forward. This is where the Bible says, "Had they known they would not have crucified the Lamb of glory."

Do you realize that you are the reason that the enemy regrets crucifying Jesus? You, believer. You, with Holy Spirit dwelling on the inside of you. Jesus told the disciples that it was better for them if He left because He knew what was coming. Do you think that maybe Jesus knows what is coming on the other side of your trial? Is it possible that perhaps He actually sees the end from the beginning? Jesus looked at the pain and torment of enduring the cross, then looked straight through to what would come after. He laid down His life because *what came after the trial was worth the pain.*

The very power of the Godhead is bodily in you with the same power that raised Christ Jesus from the dead. Satan's one problem in Jesus became millions of problems for generations to come in you, me, and every true believer that would live in the Spirit. I cannot encourage you enough to live a life where if you were the only one to ever follow after Jesus, the enemy would still regret crucifying Him. Does your life make the enemy regret crucifying Him?

Jesus said these works and greater you will do (John 14:12). It is your turn to wreak havoc on the kingdom of darkness. When God spoke to me and said, "Jessika, had the enemy known what I was going to do through this, then he wouldn't have attacked you in the first place," He was referring back to the enemy's greatest mistake of all time and his continual propensity to make this mistake.

The enemy may have struck a few punches in on you. He definitely had his fair share on me. Maybe you're in the season where everything you had dreamed for seems to fall to pieces. Perhaps life came up behind you with a baseball bat and knocked your legs out from under you. But listen to me closely: if you will not quit, God will make the enemy pay for every single place of pain. He will redeem your situation so good that the enemy will regret attacking you in the first place.

A few months after God spoke this to me, I was asked to share my testimony briefly at a conference. When it was time for prayer, I looked down the aisle to see a man walking toward me with a cane. He had on a veterans uniform. As he came closer, I saw on his hat that he had fought in the Vietnam War. He approached me with tears in his eyes and he said, "I've battled anxiety and depression every day for forty years since the war. Right after you gave your testimony, it lifted and I have hope again."

Right then, I knew that the door had been opened. What Satan had meant to destroy me was the very thing that God was going to use to thrust me forward. The very area that I had been attacked in was the very place that I would set people free. What I overcame I now had authority over to help others. I went to the side of the room, I fell to my knees, and I acknowledged what Jesus had known all along. The pain I had endured would be worth it. It wasn't about me. It was about this man. It was about forty years of struggle obliterated in a moment. I do not say this lightly: I would go through it all again just for this one man to be set free.

After David killed Goliath with a slingshot and a stone, he

took Goliath's own sword and cut his head off with it. This was exactly what David had told Goliath he would do.

> "Then David said to the Philistine, 'You come to me with a sword, a spear, and a javelin, but I come to you in the name of the Lord of Hosts, the God of the armies of Israel, whom you have taunted. This day the Lord will deliver you into my hands, and I will strike you down and remove your head from you.'" (1 Samuel 17:45)

The sword that was meant to kill David was literally the same sword he used to slaughter his enemy. Do you understand? The weapon that was meant to knock you down will be the one that God uses to lift you up. That battle that should have made you quit, that one that you still cringe when you think of, the one that still brings tears to your eyes.. oh, my friend, how Jesus will use that very thing and let you destroy the enemy with it. What could be more humiliating than that? What you meant to break me, I will use to set many others free. Every ounce of my roaring woman gets fired up just thinking about it.

The story does not stop there. Years later, when David was having to flee Saul, he found himself with Ahimelech the priest. David needed a weapon and it just so happens that the only sword Ahimelech could give him was the sword that was used to cut off Goliath's head.

God put that sword back in David's hands to bring victory in his next season. In other words, the battles you're fighting in this season will produce weapons to bring about victory in your next season. Truly, "No weapon formed against you shall prosper!"

The enemy has plans to steal, kill, and destroy; however, the weapons he uses against you, God will use to destroy him. The enemy will regret attacking me; he will regret attacking you. You gain authority over what you conquer and I am going to spend my life destroying anxiety, depression, suicide, and other post trauma related symptoms. I have no doubt he already regrets messing with me and I'm only getting started. Cue some fired up power music. To the ones who didn't think I would make it through, look at ya girl now. I didn't just make it through, I conquered and I have learned the secret to enduring, the truth that God will always make the enemy pay.

Inevitably, every time I preach this message, there is someone who comes up to me afterward and asks the question, "If this is actually true, then why does Satan keep attacking people?" I understand their thinking. If God's redemptive power is this extravagant, then you think the enemy would give up. If God really could "work all things for the good of those who love Him" (Romans 8), then what is the point? The nature of the enemy is to try his best to make the body of Christ miserable, but mostly he is playing a betting game against you. His hope is that you will quit before your redemption comes. He takes the risk of having his attacks fly back in his face with the chance of you giving up. I don't know what that does to you. It ticks me off. It lights my fire. Burn, baby, burn. If you want to bet against me, then you better prepare for war.

So what about you, my friend? Are you ready to take what the enemy meant to make you quit and use it to set others free? It is time to start making him regret messing with you in the first place. In case no one has told you lately, you are a heck of a lot stronger than you think. Greater is He that is in you that He that is in the world.

17

TIME TO LET GO

MANY TIMES, THE BIGGEST HINDRANCE TO WHAT GOD WANTS TO DO is our insistence to hang onto what we *thought* He would do. To move fully into our next season, we must let go of the past and embrace the future!

Paul gives frustratingly difficult advice in Philippians when he says, "This one thing I do, forgetting what lies behind and pressing forward." This is much easier to say and not as easy to do. We must learn to leave the past behind us. It is not about who you are, what was done to you, or what mistakes you might have made. It is about the future that is ahead of you. The attacks you have faced are rarely about who you are right now; instead, they are about who the enemy knows you will become. We cannot become the person God meant us to be if we remain fixated on what was.

I tend to eventually let go of the mistakes others made and the mistakes I made, but struggle deeply to let go of what I thought God was planning to do. It's difficult to reconcile the future you saw for yourself and the place you find yourself. When your future was full of expectancy for you and your spouse, but you get a divorce. When you thought the business would flourish and now it is bankrupt. When the dream dies, we have to know it is time to let go of the dream, let go of the way we thought it would be, and allow God to restore, redeem, replace, how He sees fit.

I happen to find this the most difficult. I'm constantly looking for ways to get back to the original plan when instead I need to be asking God for the new plan. I begin to wonder if He has a new plan at all. It's comical in light of who He is. He has sat on the throne guiding the life of humanity for generations and has yet to find a situation that made Him worry. The all too familiar Jeremiah 29:11 comes to mind: "'For I know the plans I have for you,' declares the Lord." Notice that *plans* is plural. In other words, if you happen to mess this one up, it's okay, He has a back up plan. This is evident in the reality that before the foundations of the earth, Christ was crucified. Before Eve ever touched the fruit, Jesus had a plan for how to redeem the situation. Let me assure you, before this season of trials came into your life, God already had a plan for how He would redeem what was stolen. He is not afraid. He is not wondering how He will recover your life. He is not upset thinking that you ruined it all. He is certainly not thinking the enemy has stopped His intentions. He has a plan. Now we just need to get on board with His plan.

A question I ask God when things seem to fall apart is, "How are you planning to redeem this?" I want to know what He's doing, not just what the enemy is doing. I want to know where we're going, so that I can follow His leading there. I don't want to keep trudging along the old path if Jesus has started walking in a different direction. What a tragedy if you are now on the other side of your trial and you keep fighting for the old thing when God is wanting to do a new thing.

It is not my job to fix every mess; it is my responsibility to yield to the One who is really good at fixing things. So many times in our attempt to "clean our mess," we're really just holding on to how we wanted life to go. As you know by now, life will not always go the way you think it will. It won't always go the way you thought He said it would. Like Paul, we need to learn to be flexible. We have to let go of what was and look to Jesus to guide us forward. I have a friend who says that most of us are looking for a map when God gave us a Guide instead. We have to stop following the map and start talking to the Guide.

When all was said and done, I had to let go of how I thought my life was going to be. Previous to PTSD, I had my idea of what I would be doing, where I would be doing it, and who I would be doing it with for many years to come. Then, in a flash, everything was gone. I wasn't doing the same thing, I wasn't in the same place, and I didn't have the same people around me. The truth was, that season was over. I was doing new things in new places, with new people, but I spent so much time trying to regain what was lost that I didn't recognize that God was providing something new. I spoke earlier about God being the great Exchanger; it is so necessary that we learn what God is wanting to repair and what He is wanting to exchange. There will be times that He wants to repair what broke, but there are many times He just wants to exchange it.

When we hold onto our idea of how things should be, we prolong the redemption process. It is time to let go. Decide to focus on what is in your hands right now, not what *was* in your hands. Focus on what God is saying right now. It's a new season, a new beginning; embrace the new. It is time to trust our Guide. I've said it throughout this book, but I will continue to say it all of my days: God is intent on building a relationship with you built on trust. He is trustworthy. You cannot lose anything that is necessary for your future. God is the Master Redeemer, so let Him redeem your life. Totally surrender how you thought it should be and let Him do exceedingly, abundantly more than you could ask, think, or imagine.

18

REDEFINING SUCCESS

I WAS SITTING IN MY FIRST YEAR CLASS AT BETHEL SCHOOL OF Supernatural Ministry and our pastor, Bill Johnson, was speaking. I do not even remember what he was talking about until he turned to Judges 20 and began to read to us. I'll paraphrase. The Israelites wanted to go to war and they went to God and asked Him if they should go. The Lord told them to go to battle. They went and they lost. They came back to God and asked Him again if they should go to battle. Again, the Lord told them to go and again they lost. A third time, they returned to the Lord and asked if they should go to war, and a third time, God tells them to go, but this time He tells them that He will deliver their enemies into their hands. After obeying God and losing the battle twice, they finally win the battle.

Bill finishes reading and shuts his Bible. He looks out and he simply says, "God defines success differently than we do."

Many people have been told they had failed or that they must have missed God. You've been told that it is your failure that caused the difficult situations you're in. In Judges 20, it was not failure to God that the Israelites lost the battle! In fact, He instructed them to go into the battle knowing it would not turn out how they thought it would. And yet, they were successful to God because they kept coming back to ask Him what to do, even when they had just lost the battle.

In this moment, Holy Spirit whispered to me and said, "Jessika, you haven't failed Me. You're still here today when you could have quit." It still brings tears to my eyes. God did not see me as a failure. I had. Maybe even others had. If you're reading this book, you have not failed. No matter what you have heard, you have not failed because you are still seeking His heart. You have not failed because you are still running after Him even though it has been hard. You would not be reading this book if that were not true. Going through a hard time does not necessarily indicate that you missed God. Just because things did not turn out the way you assumed they should does not necessarily mean you missed God. Everything going according to our plans is not evidence of Kingdom Success.

So many people told me that I must have missed God when I went to the Congo. People told me that if I would have listened to Him, then I would not have been in the condition I was in. I truly believed that I must have sinned or misheard, because I would not have PTSD if I had obeyed Him. These thoughts and words penetrated deep. They solidified my deepest fears and beliefs about myself. I was a horrible failure.

For almost a year, I had carried the burden of being a massive screw up. My choices had hurt the people I cared the most about. My choices had almost cost me my life. I thought I had ruined all my chances of ever going back on the mission field. I thought I would never get to preach another sermon. I had decided I was willing to spend the rest of my life stacking chairs in the church just to be able to serve because I thought I had lost the privilege of ever being in ministry again. To sum it up, I thought I was disqualified.

Then God spoke His Truth. I was not a failure, because I had not quit. Nothing and no one can replace those words. The moments where God Himself shows up and speaks truth directly to you mark you forever. It no longer mattered what everyone else had thought or said about me. He spoke. I was not a failure. Listen to me: you are not a failure. Right now, if you are reading this and you can identify with these fears and doubts, I want you to stop here.

Take a moment and turn your attention toward Him. Ask Him what He thinks about that situation. Ask Him what He is saying about you. Listen until He speaks. Do not change the subject. You do not need to know what I said. You do not need to know what Bill said. You certainly do not need to know what all the people around you have said. You need to know what He says. Take your time and hear His truth.

Please understand, I am in no way saying that I handled everything correctly, as you have already seen throughout this book. I am not even saying that I was not the cause of some of my own pain, and I absolutely was the cause of pain for others. I'm not saying you haven't made any mistakes. I'm saying that just because what you're dealing with feels like failure, does not mean that God considers *you* a failure.

Someone reading this right now needs to forgive themselves. You need to let go of the shame and guilt of perceived failure. You need to understand that no matter what happened, whether it was your fault or not is irrelevant. God says, you have not failed because you still came back to Him. You have not quit. Success is running to Him even when things didn't turn out the way you thought they would. Success is trust and dependence even in the face of defeat or disappointment. We need to realize that heaven measures success differently. If you do not quit, you win.

What do you think the Israelites were thinking when they lost the first battle? Thoughts of confusion and doubt. Perhaps wondering if God had abandoned them. I cannot imagine the amount of mental attack that would have come rushing in. Their response? Go back to the One who had led them into their losing battle.

It seems illogical. Still, once again, they return and, once again, they receive the instruction to battle. A second loss. The bewilderment. The feeling of desperation. The mourning of loss. Remember that in the very beginning of this book, I told you that God is leading all of us in a journey of trust. What is the response of our heart when it appears that the One who was supposed to be the most trustworthy leads us into what seems as ultimate defeat?

Friend, it does not matter how many "defeats" you've experienced. It doesn't matter how long this battle has been going on. In this journey of trust, success is gauged way differently than our natural mind can conceive. We must lean into the Spirit. Go back to Him and ask Him again. You will succeed. If you do not quit, you win.

EPILOGUE

AFTER I WAS HEALED, I FELT THE NUDGE OF HOLY SPIRIT DIRECTING me back toward Congo. I spoke with the team that ran the ministry there and found out I could go back that summer. I was excited and I was scared. I knew it was something I had to do. I was determined that fear would not rule me. I reached out to mentors and asked for prayer and covering. I had spent years doing ministry as a loner and I knew that this time around, I wanted to do it different. One year after I moved to California, I was on a plane back to Africa for a short trip. I knew we would soon find out just how healed I really was. Hopefully, this was Jesus and not my stubborn fighter coming out.

As soon as I crossed over the border and breathed in that Congolese air, I wanted to burst into tears. Again, it still felt like home. It was so unexplainable after everything that had taken place. My heart was full, when I thought it should be scared. I was taking in every sight and every sound, so grateful that I was able to return to this place that I loved. Just a year earlier, I did not even know if I would survive, and truth be told, without divine intervention, I would have just taken care of that myself.

The very first night I was there, an all too familiar sound rang out. POP! POP! POP! Three quick shots and then silence. I hadn't heard live gunshots in over a year. I knew the risk I was taking when I made the decision to come back. I mean, really though, what the heck. The first stinking night. Couldn't Jesus offer me some sort of grace period? Like, hey, here's 24 hours for you to reacclimate to being in a war zone.

I sat still, waiting to see if the shots would continue. Nothing came. I eventually remembered that I had brought a friend with me and turned to check on her. She was still fast asleep.

I rolled back over and whispered to Jesus, or maybe just to myself, "I feel nothing." I knew then that not only had I been healed, I had been transformed. There was no trace of the trauma wounds that had plagued me. There was no fear or insecurity. God truly can heal you so well that it feels like it happened to someone else. That's often how I feel when I tell my testimony. I describe the suicidal mess that I was and it's hard for me to even identify with that person anymore. I'll recount moments during that period and it feels as if I'm telling someone else's story. No therapist can do what Jesus has done. I still love therapists, though.

When I returned home, I decided to stay in Redding, California, and continue to attend Bethel School of Supernatural Ministry. I had spent a whole year getting healed, so I wanted to see what would God do if I gave another year, while I was healthy, just to seek Him. That year during school, I started traveling again doing speaking engagements and missions. As the threat of ISIS was plastered over the world's television screens, I was wrecked to see what God wanted to do in the Middle East. I knew that as much as He wanted to turn rebel leaders into sons that He wanted to see the Sauls in the terrorist groups turned into Pauls. I began taking trips into the war torn nations of the Middle East and bringing teams with me. At the end of my second year of ministry school, I won a very special award named after our pastor's father, given to those who notably carry revival. As I walked up to receive my award, I was undone by the goodness and redemption of my Father. I came to California burnt out, suicidal, ready to quit, and now I was accepting an award as a revivalist. I kind of wanted to tell them they had made a mistake, because receiving the award almost felt comical in light of how I came. Again, only Jesus, but He wasn't done yet.

When I was nineteen years old, I had told God that I wanted to minister on every inhabited continent by the time I was thirty. One of the gifts for winning that award was an all expense paid ministry trip with our pastor to a location that they picked. It just so happened that this year that trip would be in March to Australia. As Jesus would do it, that was the very last continent that I needed to accomplish the dream I had with God since I was nineteen years old. I was on my way to Australia when I received notice that Bethel TV was releasing the testimony video of my healing at church. We had filmed the summer before and I was uncertain if or when they would choose to release it. So here I was on a free trip with someone I greatly respected, going to a nation that was fulfilling a dream I'd had for over a decade, when they release the story of my breakthrough. Then I noticed the date, March 31, 2017. It was the exact day that I had left DR-Congo four years previous.

Our God is a God of redemption. He will go to extreme measures to display His goodness, kindness, and love. He will make the enemy pay for everything that was stolen from you. Do not give up. This trial you are in is an invitation to more.

I am now ending a chapter in Redding and launching into a new adventure in Brazil. While in Redding, I started another non-profit called Yielded Ministries. I continue to travel the world preaching the Gospel of Jesus Christ and encouraging the church to get out of their comfort zone. We do many projects reaching out to the broken in some of the darkest situations of injustice. We have work in Venezuela and Northern Brazil working directly with those affected by a massive humanitarian crises inside Venezuela. I've seen countless people healed of anxiety, depression, and post traumatic stress disorder. I'm still doing my best to take off the church mask, but more importantly than anything I've ever done or will do, I am still madly in love with Jesus and trust Him more than I ever have. I'd say He's still making the enemy pay for the months he stole. Undoubtedly, more trials will come, in my life and in yours, but we will choose joy. We will choose joy because we know on the other side of adversity is a breakthrough that makes the pain worth it.

ABOUT THE AUTHOR

Jessika Tate is an international speaker, missionary, author, and shameless coffee lover who has been traveling the world preaching the Gospel and doing aide projects for over a decade. She has followed the call to go into some of the darkest places on earth including war zones in the Middle East and Africa, prisons, brothels, and anywhere that desperately needs the light of Jesus. She is passionate about inspiring people to fall in love with Jesus, equipping the church to fully yield their lives and walk in the power of the Holy Spirit. Jessika is the founder of Yielded Ministries, a nonprofit organization that focuses on providing aide and advocacy for communities in unjust and vulnerable situations. She currently resides in Sao Jose dos Campos, Brazil where she teaches in a local ministry college, oversees Yielded projects in Venezuela and Brazil, as well as continues to travel, encouraging the church to get out of their comfort zones and love others well.

FOR MORE INFORMATION, CONNECT ONLINE AT:

🌐 **YIELDEDMINISTRIES.COM**